BIBLICAL BEGINNINGS
FOR PRESCHOOLERS

P.L.P.
Parent Lesson Planner

 Weekly Lesson Schedule

 Lesson Instructions

 Master Supply Lists

 Coloring Pages

First printing: May 2015

Master Books®, P.O. Box 726, Green Forest, AR 72638

Master Books® is a division of the New Leaf Publishing Group, Inc.

ISBN: 978-0-89051-885-4

Printed in the United States of America

Please visit our website for other great titles:
www.masterbooks.com

For information regarding author interviews,
please contact the publicity department at (870) 438-5288.

Master Books®
A Division of New Leaf Publishing Group
www.masterbooks.com

Where Creation Inspires Education

Since 1975, Master Books has been providing educational resources based on a biblical worldview to students of all ages. At the heart of these resources is our firm belief in a literal six-day creation, a young earth, the global Flood as revealed in Genesis 1–11, and other vital evidence to help build a critical foundation of scriptural authority for everyone. By equipping students with biblical truths and their key connection to the world of science and history, it is our hope they will be able to defend their faith in a skeptical, fallen world.

If the foundations are destroyed, what can the righteous do?
Psalm 11:3; NKJV

As the largest publisher of creation science materials in the world, Master Books is honored to partner with our authors and educators, including:

Ken Ham of Answers in Genesis

Michael Farris of the Home School Legal Defense Association

Dr. John Morris and Dr. Jason Lisle of the Institute for Creation Research

Dr. Donald DeYoung and Michael Oard of the Creation Research Society

Dr. James Stobaugh, John Hudson Tiner, Rick and Marilyn Boyer, Dr. Tom DeRosa, Todd Friel, Israel Wayne, and so many more!

Whether a pre-school learner or a scholar seeking an advanced degree, we offer a wonderful selection of award-winning resources for all ages and educational levels.

But sanctify the Lord God in your hearts, and always be ready
to give a defense to everyone who asks you a reason for the hope
that is in you, with meekness and fear.
1 Peter 3:15; NKJV

Permission to Copy

Lessons for a 36-week course!

Overview: This *Biblical Beginnings for Preschoolers* PLP contains materials for use with *God Made the World & Me, A is for Adam, D is for Dinosaur, N is for Noah, Big Thoughts for Little Thinker* series, and *Noah's Ark Pre-School Activity Book*. Materials are organized by each book in the following sections:

📄	Master Supply Lists
📑	Daily Plans and Instructions
✏️	Coloring Pages

Features: Each suggested weekly schedule has four easy-to-manage lessons that combine reading, coloring pages, activities, and vocabulary-building opportunities for students aged 3 to 5. Pages in this PLP are perforated, making them easy to tear out, hand out, grade, and store. As always, you are encouraged to adjust the schedule and materials as you need to in order to best work within your educational program.

Workflow: Parents can follow the included lesson schedule and help their student complete each of the daily course materials or activities. Upon completion of each day's work, parents can indicate it in the schedule. Young students may need to go over the course material more than once to aid comprehension, and parents have flexibility in how they choose to do so in order to meet the needs of their individual student.

Lesson Scheduling: Space is given for assignment dates. There is flexibility in scheduling. Each week listed has four days, but due to vacations, the schoolwork week may not be M-TH. Please adapt the days to your school schedule. As the student completes each assignment, you may put an "X" in the box.

🕐	Approximately 45 minutes to an hour per lesson, four days a week
🔑	Weekly lesson schedule, daily instructions, master supply lists and coloring pages are included
📑	Science, art, music, and physical activities are part of this course
♻️	Materials allow integration of basic skills learning with biblical themes and history
✏️	Designed for ages 3 to 5 in a one year course
📄	Supports activity-based learning

God Made the World and Me

Take a fun and educational journey through songs, science, and fun art projects as you learn about the creation week and develop a basic understanding of the world.

A is for Adam, D is for Dinosaur, N is for Noah

A unique, easel book series for learning the alphabet with colorful rhymes and illustrations, along with important biblical facts and helpful information for parents.

Noah's Ark Pre-School Activity Book

Learn shapes, colors, numbers, opposites, and more with puzzles, connect the dots, and other fun activities, all built around learning more about Noah's Ark!

Big Thoughts for Little Thinkers

Teach age-appropriate biblical concepts like the gospel, the Trinity, the mission, and God's Word as Scripture in this delightfully illustrated series.

Contents

Teacher Helpers

This course was designed to be used with 3-, 4-, and 5-year-olds. Please adjust all activities and assignments according to the needs and abilities of your students.

Most lessons include activities for elementary-age students. If the whole family wants to be involved, older students can help younger students complete the activities.

Coloring pages included in this Parent Lesson Planner are front and back. If you prefer to print them out as single sheets, please go to: www.masterbooks.com/free-downloads; scroll down to the links below "Coloring Pages." There are four pdfs that can be downloaded to your computer and printed as needed.

We have provided a helpful materials list. We suggest preparing in nine-week increments, but certainly at least a week in advance. We suggest using a plastic container to keep the needed supplies in one place. Students love to be in charge of retrieving the necessary items for each day.

Encourage students at the end of each day to clean up and return supplies to the container and put away their books, pencils, and crayons.

God Made the World & Me

- This book uses the *Creation Story for Children* books.

- Use the "Dear Parents" pages as a review of the week and preparation for the next week.

- Instructors should use discretion with how many and which Learning Center options are completed. The attention span and age of students should be the guide.

A is for Adam, D is for Dinosaur, and N is for Noah

- *N is for Noah* has many activities that are repeated from *A is for Adam* and *D is for Dinosaur*. Children this age love repetition and will remember important lessons by repeating activities.

- We recommend repeating as many activities as possible, but instructors may opt to simply review repeated activities and discuss what was learned.

- Students are regularly asked to repeat a section back to you. This is called narration. Students should not be expected to recite the section word for word, but should include key concepts. Students will get better at narration with practice. We suggest instructors avoid giving students a second chance at narrating a section. This will teach the student to listen carefully the first time.

- Students should practice writing each letter with their finger in the air. Letters should be large.

- Students may also be given the opportunity to write each letter on a piece of paper. Each letter should be large enough to take up the entire sheet of paper. Young students may use the "fist" hold but should be encouraged to try holding the pencil or crayon the proper way. A "gripper" may be used to help the student learn the proper placement in his or her hand.

- Let students name other words that begin with the letter you are working on. Instructors may want to write the words on the letter sheets drawn by the student. Another option is to cut out pictures from catalogs or magazines of items that begin with the letter being worked on. The pictures may be glued onto the letter sheets.

- Letters may also be practiced by forming them with play dough, writing them in sand, or writing them on a cookie sheet with shaving cream. Be creative and come up with your own activities.

Noah's Ark Pre-school Activity Book

- Continue to practice the concepts during the day. For example, practice colors by pointing to various items and asking the student what color it is. Ask the student to identify items around the house with the same shapes they are learning.

- Instructors may want to help the student do further research on animals mentioned in the book. Library books, *44 Animals of the Bible*, *The World of Animals* available at MasterBooks.com, or websites such as AnswersinGenesis.org.

Big Thoughts for Little Thinkers

- Let each book be used as a springboard for conversation.

- Encourage students to ask questions. Offer simple answers. Read Scripture verses to help explain difficult concepts.

- Students may be encouraged to draw pictures based on a Scripture verse or concept covered.

- Remember to take time to pray with students.

- Dinner time is a good time to continue the conversation with the entire family.

God Made The World & Me

Week 1/Lesson 1

Physical Center
- ☐ flashlights

Science Center #1
- ☐ flashlight
- ☐ a prism

Science Center #2
- ☐ tub of water
- ☐ cornstarch
- ☐ towels for cleanup

Art Center
- ☐ half sheets of black or dark blue construction paper
- ☐ drinking straws for each student
- ☐ white tempera paint
- ☐ silver glitter (optional)

Older Students
- ☐ flashlight
- ☐ cardstock
- ☐ books
- ☐ scissors

Younger Students
- ☐ half sheets of black or dark blue construction paper
- ☐ white tempera or finger paint
- ☐ white pencil or chalk
- ☐ spoon to scoop paint
- ☐ paint smocks
- ☐ water
- ☐ towels

Magazine COLOR Collage
- ☐ assortment of magazines
- ☐ scissors
- ☐ glue sticks
- ☐ 11"x17" white paper

Easy Finger Paint
- ☐ 2 cups white flour
- ☐ 2 cups cold water
- ☐ food coloring

Week 2/Lesson 2

Science Center
- ☐ your graph of the different kinds of sky
- ☐ a marker
- ☐ books and/or pictures about weather or various skies (we recommend *Big Book of Earth and Sky* available at MasterBooks.com)

Art Center #1
- ☐ half sheets of light blue construction paper
- ☐ cotton balls
- ☐ glue sticks
- ☐ pictures of various skies

Art Center #2
- ☐ construction paper
- ☐ crayons or markers
- ☐ music with "weather sounds"

Older Students
- ☐ clear glass jar with a lid
- ☐ cup of hot water
- ☐ warming tray
- ☐ *Creation Big Book*
- ☐ (Optional: aluminum pie pan filled with ice cubes)

Younger Students
- ☐ half sheets of light blue construction paper
- ☐ cotton balls
- ☐ glue sticks
- ☐ pictures of various skies

A Sky Full of AIR
- ☐ a balloon

Week 3/Lesson 3

Physical Center #1
- ☐ bubble solution
- ☐ upbeat music

Physical Center #2
- ☐ use furniture in room for obstacle course

Science Center
- ☐ plastic tub to hold water
- ☐ a variety of containers that will NOT float
- ☐ some "sink and float" items
- ☐ towels for cleanup
- ☐ a large pitcher (or two) of water

Art Center
- ☐ construction paper
- ☐ crayons
- ☐ paintbrushes
- ☐ blue wash (diluted blue tempera paint)
- ☐ plastic tablecloth

Older Students
- ☐ your file cards with words listing the ways you use water
- ☐ your graph with the children's names
- ☐ markers
- ☐ a glass jar filled with tap water
- ☐ a bottle of fresh water

Younger Students
- ☐ use the Science Center and its supplies or set up a separate water table with plastic containers

Bubble Fun
- ☐ a piece of cotton string about 3 to 4 feet long
- ☐ bubble solution

Materials List

Week 4/Lesson 4

Physical Center #1
- ☐ a plastic tablecloth to protect the floor
- ☐ a tub of sand, dirt, or potting soil
- ☐ garden hand shovels
- ☐ containers for filling and pouring out sand

Physical Center #2
- ☐ rocks
- ☐ masking tape

Science Center
- ☐ magnifying glasses
- ☐ many different kinds of rocks
- ☐ small containers of water
- ☐ eyedroppers
- ☐ a small food scale
- ☐ a balance scale (to weigh and compare rocks)

Art Center
- ☐ a small plastic container (empty butter, cream cheese, or yogurt container) for each child
- ☐ three colors of aquarium rocks
- ☐ a lot of liquid glue
- ☐ a bowl
- ☐ several sturdy spoons

Older Students
- ☐ a variety of rocks
- ☐ several nails

Younger Students
- ☐ dirt (maybe some sand)
- ☐ rocks
- ☐ scoops
- ☐ spoons
- ☐ buckets
- ☐ containers

Week 5/Lesson 5

Physical Center
- ☐ a variety of fruits and vegetables

Science Center #1
- ☐ vegetable peelers
- ☐ plastic knives
- ☐ two large bowls
- ☐ small paper bowls
- ☐ plastic spoons or forks

Science Center #2
- ☐ packets of seeds
- ☐ plastic bags for seeds

Science Center #3
- ☐ plastic cups
- ☐ potting soil
- ☐ scoop or old spoons
- ☐ seeds
- ☐ craft sticks
- ☐ marker

Art Center
- ☐ construction paper
- ☐ two or three colors of tempera paint
- ☐ pie plates for the paint
- ☐ vegetables you cut up ahead of time
- ☐ baby wipes

Younger Students
- ☐ half sheets of light blue construction paper
- ☐ glue sticks
- ☐ a variety of precut paper flowers and stems

Thank You, God, for Plants
- ☐ a platter
- ☐ one pineapple
- ☐ two oranges
- ☐ four tomatoes
- ☐ six green apples
- ☐ eight bananas
- ☐ ten purple grapes

God Made Flowers
- ☐ one or two long-stemmed carnations
- ☐ clear glass vase
- ☐ green food coloring

Play Dough Flowers
- ☐ play dough of various colors
- ☐ wax paper
- ☐ cloth or paper towels
- ☐ basin of soapy water for cleanup

Pin a Petal on the Flower
- ☐ large sheet of yellow construction paper
- ☐ other colored construction paper to cut out "petals" about a foot long
- ☐ scissors
- ☐ tape
- ☐ marker

Sorting Flowers
- ☐ a low table
- ☐ an assortment of plastic or real flowers
- ☐ several vases or pots

Week 6/Lesson 6

Physical Center #1
- ☐ a poster or pictures of the moon

Science Center #1
- ☐ sunshine (or a flashlight)
- ☐ several 3–D objects

Science Center #2
- ☐ glow in the dark stars
- ☐ pictures of constellations

Materials List

Art Center
- [ ] black or blue construction paper
- [ ] star stickers
- [ ] white or yellow chalk

Younger Students
- [ ] blue or black construction paper
- [ ] chalk
- [ ] star stickers
- [ ] half sheets of black or blue construction paper

Older Students
- [ ] sponges cut in the shape of stars, crescent moons, and/or circles
- [ ] white and yellow tempera paint
- [ ] pie tins
- [ ] paint smocks or shirts
- [ ] water
- [ ] towels

Make Hand Shadows
- [ ] a white wall or a white sheet
- [ ] bright lamp

Week 7/Lesson 7

Science Center #1
- [ ] seashells and/or plastic sea creatures
- [ ] a tub of water
- [ ] a plastic tablecloth
- [ ] towels

Science Center #2
- [ ] five to eight seashells on a tray
- [ ] sand dollar
- [ ] a cloth

Art Center
- [ ] a small whole fish or two from the local market
- [ ] slightly diluted tempera paints
- [ ] paintbrushes
- [ ] washcloth

- [ ] tub of water
- [ ] baby wipes
- [ ] construction paper

Older Students
- [ ] two to four seashells
- [ ] drawing paper
- [ ] pencils
- [ ] markers

Younger Students
- [ ] construction paper
- [ ] clear contact paper
- [ ] various colors of tissue paper
- [ ] large wiggly eyes for fish

Week 8/Lesson 8

Physical Center #2
- [ ] a book with pictures of various kinds of birds

Science Center #1
- [ ] feathers

Science Center #2
- [ ] a flat pan with a variety of birdseed
- [ ] magnifying glasses
- [ ] tweezers
- [ ] muffin tin

Art Center #1
- [ ] precut shapes (circles, ovals, triangles)
- [ ] glue sticks
- [ ] construction paper
- [ ] feathers
- [ ] birdseed

Art Center #2
- [ ] construction paper
- [ ] crayons
- [ ] scissors
- [ ] glue

Older Students
- [ ] straw
- [ ] mud
- [ ] small sticks
- [ ] string
- [ ] paper bowls

Younger Students
- [ ] a bowl
- [ ] a raw egg
- [ ] several boiled eggs

Five Little Birds
- [ ] five flat wooden sticks
- [ ] crayons or markers

Week 9/Lesson 9

Physical Center #1
- [ ] an assortment of stuffed animals or pictures of animals or library books of animals

Science Center
- [ ] a plastic tub with some dirt in it
- [ ] cornmeal
- [ ] four or five worms
- [ ] black and white construction paper
- [ ] a flashlight

Art Center
- [ ] construction paper
- [ ] magazines for cutting
- [ ] scissors
- [ ] glue sticks

Older/Younger Students
- [ ] books from the library about different animals

Older/Younger Students
- [ ] books with pictures of animals

Materials List

Week 10/Lesson 10

Physical Center #1
- [ ] blindfolds (cloth hair bands work well)

Science Center
- [ ] dolls
- [ ] small pictures of boys and girls
- [ ] a large graph with squares on which to put the pictures
- [ ] scotch tape
- [ ] knife
- [ ] jelly beans in clear glass jar

Art Center
- [ ] small plain paper plates or circles of various skin tones
- [ ] markers
- [ ] yarn
- [ ] glue sticks
- [ ] mirrors

Younger Students
- [ ] dolls
- [ ] props for playing house

Week 11/Lesson 11

Physical Center #1
- [ ] optional: alarm clock
- [ ] Optional: CD of peaceful music

Science Center
- [ ] tub of warm water with plastic sea creatures and seashells
- [ ] towels
- [ ] a plastic tablecloth

Art Center
- [ ] paper plates
- [ ] jumbo craft sticks
- [ ] tape
- [ ] markers

Older Students
- [ ] pictures of different kinds of animals

- [ ] a large book on animals (Include animals who sleep at night and those who sleep during the day.) We recommend *44 Animals of the Bible*; *The World of Animals* available at MasterBooks.com.

Younger Students
- [ ] dolls and props for playing house
- [ ] hand towel for doll blankets
- [ ] blanket/sleeping bag for children

Take Time for Creativity
- [ ] construction paper
- [ ] old magazines
- [ ] various stickers of animals, birds, insects, etc.
- [ ] scissors
- [ ] glue

A Resting Game
- [ ] a fancy gift bag
- [ ] a variety of fruits and vegetables
- [ ] a large platter
- [ ] toothpicks

Week 12/Lesson 12

Physical Center #2
- [ ] animal crackers

Science Center
- [ ] a variety of fabric pieces (heavier threads to pull out)
- [ ] magnifying glasses
- [ ] tweezers

Art Center
- [ ] a variety of pieces of fabric
- [ ] construction paper
- [ ] markers and glue
- [ ] blackboard
- [ ] chalk

Older Students
- [ ] strips of construction paper
- [ ] whole pieces of construction paper
- [ ] tape

God Made Me!
- [ ] magnifying glass
- [ ] ink pads
- [ ] paper
- [ ] pencils and/or markers

Creation MOBILE
- [ ] colored pencils
- [ ] scissors
- [ ] tape or glue
- [ ] assorted yarn or ribbon
- [ ] coat hanger

Week 13/Lesson 13

Physical Center #1
- [ ] box of crackers
- [ ] chairs to move around

Physical Center #2
- [ ] animal crackers

Science Center
- [ ] precut pictures of fish, animals, and birds on stiff paper
- [ ] three baskets labeled: fins, feathers, and fur

Art Center
- [ ] construction paper — cut out a blue circle for each child
- [ ] animal crackers
- [ ] markers
- [ ] glue sticks

Materials List

Older Students
- [ ] one picture each of animals God made
- [ ] tape

Younger Students
- [ ] party hats and supplies
- [ ] a bowl of orange sections or other fruit of your choice
- [ ] sliced star fruit
- [ ] goldfish crackers
- [ ] animal crackers
- [ ] construction paper small cards with numbers 1–7 on each

Physical Center #1
- [ ] box of crackers
- [ ] chairs to move around

Physical Center #2
- [ ] animal crackers

Science Center
- [ ] precut pictures of fish, animals, and birds on stiff paper
- [ ] three baskets labeled: fins, feathers, and fur

Art Center
- [ ] construction paper — cut out a blue circle for each child
- [ ] animal crackers
- [ ] markers
- [ ] glue sticks

Older Students
- [ ] one picture each of animals God made
- [ ] tape

Younger Students
- [ ] party hats and supplies
- [ ] a bowl of orange sections or other fruit of your choice
- [ ] sliced star fruit

- [ ] goldfish crackers
- [ ] animal crackers
- [ ] construction paper small cards with numbers 1–7 on each

A is for Adam

Week 1, Day 1
- [ ] plan a trip to the zoo and/or a book with pictures of animals and people

C is for Creatures

Week 1, Day 3
- [ ] books or websites with information and photos of different kinds of animals. We recommend *44 Animals of the Bible*; *The World of Animals* available at MasterBooks.com.

E is for Eve

Week 2, Day 1
- [ ] family wedding photos or paper to draw a picture of your family

F is for Fruit

Week 2, Day 2
- [ ] plain white paper
- [ ] a puppet

G is for Ghastly

Week 2, Day 3
- [ ] plain white paper
- [ ] crayons

J is for Jovial

Week 3, Day 2
- [ ] paper for writing a letter

K is for Knew

Week 3, Day 3
- [ ] construction paper
- [ ] glue or tape
- [ ] leaves

L is for Lord

Week 3, Day 4
- [ ] a rosebush growing in your yard or a friendly neighbor's yard
- [ ] flowers growing in your yard or a friendly neighbor's yard

M is for Moan

Week 4, Day 1
- [ ] a flower or vegetable bed to weed

O is for Offering

Week 4, Day 3
- [ ] leaves
- [ ] paper doll
- [ ] plain white paper

R is for Rough

Week 5, Day 2
- [ ] three things you use to do something or as a tool (e.g., pencil, toothbrush, remote control)
- [ ] plain white paper
- [ ] magazines that show how seeds become plants that produce vegetables or fruit (to cut out)

S is for Seventy

Week 5, Day 3
- [ ] family pictures to look at
- [ ] copies of family pictures to create a family tree or draw your own pictures
- [ ] plain paper to create a family tree
- [ ] images clipped from magazines that show different people, different ages, and different colors
- [ ] plain paper to create Adam and Eve's family tree

U is for Utterly

Week 6, Day 1
- [ ] dishpan or large bowl
- [ ] two small cups of sand
- [ ] plastic animals and small figures
- [ ] water

Materials List

V is for Violent
Week 6, Day 2
- ☐ toys to re-enact Genesis 7 and 8
- ☐ plain paper

W is for Walk
Week 6, Day 3
- ☐ an animal fossil or a picture of one
- ☐ plain paper

X is for eXplode
Week 6, Day 4
- ☐ small boxes or wooden blocks
- ☐ small dollhouse
- ☐ dolls and other items to fit in and fill the dollhouse

Y is for Yes
Week 7, Day 1
- ☐ a library book written in a language you cannot read

Z is for Zip
Week 7, Day 2
- ☐ index cards
- ☐ plain paper

D is for Dinosaur
A is for Answers
Week 1, Day 1
- ☐ large sheet of paper (or several small sheets and tape) to be used through lesson "F"

J means Just awful
Week 3, Day 2
- ☐ blocks

K is for Knowledge
Week 3, Day 3
- ☐ Bible
- ☐ dictionaries and other reference books

M is for Monster
Week 4, Day 1
- ☐ blocks to shape in the form of an archway or paper cutouts forming a sphere
- ☐ items to try to slip through the hole of the archway or sphere — include some items that will not fit

N is for Noah
Week 4, Day 2
- ☐ small toy boat
- ☐ flour
- ☐ deep pan
- ☐ small rocks
- ☐ a gallon of water

P is for Pronounce
Week 4, Day 4
- ☐ *Dinosaurs by Design* and/or other dinosaur books or websites

R is for Reasons
Week 5, Day 2
- ☐ plain paper

S is for Section
Week 5, Day 3
- ☐ large tree in your yard or a park

T is for Tales
Week 5, Day 4
- ☐ cardstock (may practice on plain paper)
- ☐ crayons
- ☐ scissors

U is for Understand
Week 6, Day 1
- ☐ books from home or the library filled with pictures of Israel and where Jesus walked

V is for how Very much
Week 6, Day 2
- ☐ a Bible

W is for Watchfulness
Week 6, Day 3
- ☐ a favorite stuffed animal
- ☐ blanket

X is in eXcited
Week 6, Day 4
- ☐ plain paper

Y is for Years
Week 7, Day 1
- ☐ 60 crayons, pencils, or popsicle sticks

N is for Noah

A is for Ark
Week 1, Day 1
(Students may complete this activity again or review and discuss what they learned.)
- ☐ a Bible

B is for Back
Week 1, Day 2
(Although a review, we highly recommend completing this activity with the student.)
- ☐ a puppet

C is for Called
Week 1, Day 3
- ☐ paper to make a list

E is for Earth
Week 2, Day 1
(Students may complete this activity again or review and discuss what they learned.)
- ☐ a flower or vegetable bed to weed

F is for Fruitful

Week 2, Day 2

(Students may complete this activity again or review the "trees" they made and discuss what they learned.)

- ☐ family pictures to look at
- ☐ copies of family pictures to create a family tree or draw your own pictures
- ☐ plain paper to create a family tree
- ☐ images clipped from magazines that show different people, different ages, and different colors
- ☐ plain paper to create Adam and Eve's family tree

G is for Grave

Week 2, Day 3

(Students may complete this activity again or review and discuss what they learned.)

- ☐ Bible
- ☐ dictionaries and other reference books

H is for Hear

Week 2, Day 4

(Students may complete this activity again or review and discuss what they learned.)

- ☐ blocks

J is for Judgment

Week 3, Day 2

- ☐ a park , very large yard, or other big, open space
- ☐ tape measure
- ☐ markers such as flags, cones, soccer balls, etc.

K is for Kept

Week 3, Day 3

(Students may complete this activity again or review and discuss what they learned.)

- ☐ large tree in your yard or a park

L is for Laughing

Week 3, Day 4

(Students may complete this activity again or review and discuss what they learned and study the timeline.)

- ☐ toys to re-enact Genesis 7
- ☐ plain paper

M is for Mighty

Week 4, Day 1

(Students may complete this activity again or review and discuss what they learned.)

- ☐ small toy boat
- ☐ flour
- ☐ deep pan
- ☐ small rocks
- ☐ a gallon of water

O is for Over

Week 4, Day 3

(Students may complete this activity again or review and discuss what they learned.)

- ☐ dishpan or large bowl
- ☐ two small cups of sand
- ☐ plastic animals and small figures
- ☐ water

P is for Pleasure

Week 4, Day 4

- ☐ plain paper

Q is for Quiet

Week 5, Day 1

- ☐ plain paper or students may give answers verbally

R is for Raven

Week 5, Day 2

- ☐ plain paper

S is for Sent

Week 5, Day 3

- ☐ supplies to grow flowers or vegetables, seeds, dirt, containers

T is for Twice

Week 5, Day 4

- ☐ plain paper

V is for Very

Week 6, Day 2

(Students may complete this activity again or review and discuss what they learned.)

- ☐ an animal fossil or a picture of one
- ☐ plain paper

W is for Wonderful

Week 6, Day 3

- ☐ plain paper
- ☐ red, orange, yellow, green, blue, indigo, and violet crayons or markers

X is in eXtensive

Week 6, Day 4

- ☐ *Dinosaurs by Design* and/or other dinosaur books or websites

Y is for Years

Week 7, Day 1

(Students may complete this activity again or review and discuss what they learned.)

- ☐ a favorite stuffed animal
- ☐ blanket

Big Thoughts For Little Thinkers

- ☐ a Bible
- ☐ plain paper
- ☐ crayons or markers

First Semester Suggested Daily Schedule

Date	Day	Assignment	Due Date	✓
		First Semester — First Quarter		
Week 1	Day 1	Lesson 1: God Creates Light • *God Made the World & Me* • (GMW) • Lesson 1, Day 1 • Page 21• Lesson Plan		
	Day 2	Lesson 1: God Creates Light • Day 2 • Page 21 • Lesson Plan		
	Day 3	Lesson 1: God Creates Light • Day 3 • Page 21 • Lesson Plan		
	Day 4	Lesson 1: God Creates Light • Day 4 • Page 21 • Lesson Plan		
	Day 5			
Week 2	Day 6	Lesson 2: God Creates Sky • Day 1 • Page 22 • Lesson Plan		
	Day 7	Lesson 2: God Creates Sky • Day 2 • Page 22 • Lesson Plan		
	Day 8	Lesson 2: God Creates Sky • Day 3 • Page 22 • Lesson Plan		
	Day 9	Lesson 2: God Creates Sky • Day 4 • Page 22 • Lesson Plan		
	Day 10			
Week 3	Day 11	Lesson 3: God Creates Water • Day 1 • Page 23 • Lesson Plan		
	Day 12	Lesson 3: God Creates Water • Day 2 • Page 23 • Lesson Plan		
	Day 13	Lesson 3: God Creates Water • Day 3 • Page 23 • Lesson Plan		
	Day 14	Lesson 3: God Creates Water • Day 4 • Page 23 • Lesson Plan		
	Day 15			
Week 4	Day 16	Lesson 4: God Creates Land • Day 1 • Page 24 • Lesson Plan		
	Day 17	Lesson 4: God Creates Land • Day 2 • Page 24 • Lesson Plan		
	Day 18	Lesson 4: God Creates Land • Day 3 • Page 24 • Lesson Plan		
	Day 19	Lesson 4: God Creates Land • Day 4 • Page 24 • Lesson Plan		
	Day 20			
Week 5	Day 21	Lesson 5: God Creates Plants • Day 1 • Page 25 • Lesson Plan		
	Day 22	Lesson 5: God Creates Plants • Day 2 • Page 25 • Lesson Plan		
	Day 23	Lesson 5: God Creates Plants • Day 3 • Page 25 • Lesson Plan		
	Day 24	Lesson 5: God Creates Plants • Day 4 • Page 25 • Lesson Plan		
	Day 25			
Week 6	Day 26	Lesson 6: God Creates Sun, Moon, Stars, and Planets • Day 1 • Page 26 • Lesson Plan		
	Day 27	Lesson 6: God Creates Sun, Moon, Stars, and Planets • Day 2 • Page 26 • Lesson Plan		
	Day 28	Lesson 6: God Creates Sun, Moon, Stars, and Planets • Day 3 • Page 26 • Lesson Plan		
	Day 29	Lesson 6: God Creates Sun, Moon, Stars, and Planets • Day 4 • Page 26 • Lesson Plan		
	Day 30			
Week 7	Day 31	Lesson 7: God Creates Sea Creatures • Day 1 • Page 27 • Lesson Plan		
	Day 32	Lesson 7: God Creates Sea Creatures • Day 2 • Page 27 • Lesson Plan		
	Day 33	Lesson 7: God Creates Sea Creatures • Day 3 • Page 27 • Lesson Plan		
	Day 34	Lesson 7: God Creates Sea Creatures • Day 4 • Page 27 • Lesson Plan		
	Day 35			

Date	Day	Assignment	Due Date	✓
Week 8	Day 36	Lesson 8: God Creates Birds • Day 1 • Page 28 • Lesson Plan		
	Day 37	Lesson 8: God Creates Birds • Day 2 • Page 28 • Lesson Plan		
	Day 38	Lesson 8: God Creates Birds • Day 3 • Page 28 • Lesson Plan		
	Day 39	Lesson 8: God Creates Birds • Day 4 • Page 28 • Lesson Plan		
	Day 40			
Week 9	Day 41	Lesson 9: God Creates Animals • Day 1 • Page 29 • Lesson Plan		
	Day 42	Lesson 9: God Creates Animals • Day 2 • Page 29 • Lesson Plan		
	Day 43	Lesson 9: God Creates Animals • Day 3 • Page 29 • Lesson Plan		
	Day 44	Lesson 9: God Creates Animals • Day 4 • Page 29 • Lesson Plan		
	Day 45			
First Semester — Second Quarter				
Week 10	Day 46	Lesson 10: God Creates People • Day 1 • Page 30 • Lesson Plan		
	Day 47	Lesson 10: God Creates People • Day 2 • Page 30 • Lesson Plan		
	Day 48	Lesson 10: God Creates People • Day 3 • Page 30 • Lesson Plan		
	Day 49	Lesson 10: God Creates People • Day 4 • Page 30 • Lesson Plan		
	Day 50			
Week 11	Day 51	Lesson 11: God Creates a Day of Rest • Day 1 • Page 31 • Lesson Plan		
	Day 52	Lesson 11: God Creates a Day of Rest • Day 2 • Page 31 • Lesson Plan		
	Day 53	Lesson 11: God Creates a Day of Rest • Day 3 • Page 31 • Lesson Plan		
	Day 54	Lesson 11: God Creates a Day of Rest • Day 4 • Page 31 • Lesson Plan		
	Day 55			
Week 12	Day 56	Lesson 12: God Created ME! • Day 1 • Page 32 • Lesson Plan		
	Day 57	Lesson 12: God Created ME! • Day 2 • Page 32 • Lesson Plan		
	Day 58	Lesson 12: God Created ME! • Day 3 • Page 32 • Lesson Plan		
	Day 59	Lesson 12: God Created ME! • Day 4 • Page 32 • Lesson Plan		
	Day 60			
Week 13	Day 61	Lesson 13: Creation Celebration! • Day 1 • Page 33 • Lesson Plan		
	Day 62	Lesson 13: Creation Celebration! • Day 2 • Page 33 • Lesson Plan		
	Day 63	Lesson 13: Creation Celebration! • Day 3 • Page 33 • Lesson Plan		
	Day 64	Lesson 13: Creation Celebration! • Day 4 • Page 33 • Lesson Plan		
	Day 65			
Week 14	Day 66	*A is for Adam* • (AFA) • Week 1, Day 1 • Page 35 • Lesson Plan		
	Day 67	B is for Bible • Week 1, Day 2 • Page 35 • Lesson Plan		
	Day 68	C is for Creatures • Week 1, Day 3 • Page 35 • Lesson Plan		
	Day 69	D is for Dinosaur • Week 1, Day 4 • Page 35 • Lesson Plan		
	Day 70			

Date	Day	Assignment	Due Date	✓
Week 15	Day 71	E is for Eve • Week 2, Day 1 • Page 36 • Lesson Plan		
	Day 72	F is for Fruit • Week 2, Day 2 • Page 36 • Lesson Plan		
	Day 73	G is for Ghastly • Week 2, Day 3 • Page 36 • Lesson Plan		
	Day 74	H is for How • Week 2, Day 4 • Page 36 • Lesson Plan		
	Day 75			
Week 16	Day 76	I is for Interested • Week 3, Day 1 • Page 37 • Lesson Plan		
	Day 77	J is for Jovial • Week 3, Day 2 • Page 37 • Lesson Plan		
	Day 78	K is for Knew • Week 3, Day 3 • Page 37 • Lesson Plan		
	Day 79	L is for Lord • Week 3, Day 4 • Page 37 • Lesson Plan		
	Day 80			
Week 17	Day 81	M is for Moan • Week 4, Day 1 • Page 38 • Lesson Plan		
	Day 82	N is for Never • Week 4, Day 2 • Page 38 • Lesson Plan		
	Day 83	O is for Offering • Week 4, Day 3 • Page 38 • Lesson Plan		
	Day 84	P is for Plan • Week 4, Day 4 • Page 38 • Lesson Plan		
	Day 85			
Week 18	Day 86	Q is for Quiet • Week 5, Day 1 • Page 39 • Lesson Plan		
	Day 87	R is for Rough • Week 5, Day 2 • Page 39 • Lesson Plan		
	Day 88	S is for Seventy • Week 5, Day 3 • Page 39 • Lesson Plan		
	Day 89	T is for Trouble • Week 5, Day 4 • Page 39 • Lesson Plan		
	Day 90			

Second Semester Suggested Daily Schedule

Date	Day	Assignment	Due Date	✓
		Second Semester — Third Quarter		
Week 19	Day 91	U is for Utterly • Week 6, Day 1 • Page 40 • Lesson Plan		
	Day 92	V is for Violent • Week 6, Day 2 • Page 40• Lesson Plan		
	Day 93	W is for Walk • Week 6, Day 3 • Page 40 • Lesson Plan		
	Day 94	X is for eXplode • Week 6, Day 4 • Page 40 • Lesson Plan		
	Day 95			
Week 20	Day 96	Y is for Yes • Week 7, Day 1 • Page 41 • Lesson Plan		
	Day 97	Z is for Zip• Week 7, Day 2 • Page 41 • Lesson Plan		
	Day 98	*A is for Adam* Review • Week 7, Day 3 • Page 41 • Lesson Plan		
	Day 99	*A is for Adam* Review • Week 7, Day 4 • Page 41• Lesson Plan		
	Day 100			
Week 21	Day 101	*D is for Dinosaur* • (DFD) • A is for Answers • Week 1, Day 1 • Page 43 • Lesson Plan		
	Day 102	B is for Bible • Week 1, Day 2 • Page 43 • Lesson Plan		
	Day 103	C is for Continent • Week 1, Day 3 • Page 43 • Lesson Plan		
	Day 104	D is for Dinosaur • Week 1, Day 4 • Page 43 • Lesson Plan		
	Day 105			
Week 22	Day 106	E is for Everything • Week 2, Day 1 • Page 44 • Lesson Plan		
	Day 107	F is for Fantastic • Week 2, Day 2 • Page 44 • Lesson Plan		
	Day 108	G is for Garden • Week 2, Day 3 • Page 44 • Lesson Plan		
	Day 109	H is for Hungry • Week 2, Day 4 • Page 44 • Lesson Plan		
	Day 110			
Week 23	Day 111	I is in the middle of Sin • Week 3, Day 1 • Page 45 • Lesson Plan		
	Day 112	J means Just awful • Week 3, Day 2 • Page 45 • Lesson Plan		
	Day 113	K is for Knowledge • Week 3, Day 3 • Page 45 • Lesson Plan		
	Day 114	L is for Listen • Week 3, Day 4 • Page 45 • Lesson Plan		
	Day 115			
Week 24	Day 116	M is for Monster • Week 4, Day 1 • Page 46 • Lesson Plan		
	Day 117	N is for Noah • Week 4, Day 2 • Page 46 • Lesson Plan		
	Day 118	O is for Out • Week 4, Day 3 • Page 46 • Lesson Plan		
	Day 119	P is for Pronounce • Week 4, Day 4 • Page 46 • Lesson Plan		
	Day 120			
Week 25	Day 121	Q is for Question • Week 5, Day 1 • Page 47 • Lesson Plan		
	Day 122	R is for Reasons • Week 5, Day 2 • Page 47 • Lesson Plan		
	Day 123	S is for Section • Week 5, Day 3 • Page 47 • Lesson Plan		
	Day 124	T is for Tales • Week 5, Day 4 • Page 47 • Lesson Plan		
	Day 125			

Date	Day	Assignment	Due Date	✓
Week 26	Day 126	U is for Understand • Week 6, Day 1 • Page 48 • Lesson Plan		
	Day 127	V is for how Very much • Week 6, Day 2 • Page 48 • Lesson Plan		
	Day 128	W is for Watchfulness • Week 6, Day 3 • Page 48 • Lesson Plan		
	Day 129	X is in eXcited • Week 6, Day 4 • Page 48 • Lesson Plan		
	Day 130			
Week 27	Day 131	Y is for Years • Week 7, Day 1 • Page 49 • Lesson Plan		
	Day 132	Z is for Zeal • Week 7, Day 2 • Page 49 • Lesson Plan		
	Day 133	*D is for Dinosaur* Review • Week 7, Day 3 • Page 49 • Lesson Plan		
	Day 134	*D is for Dinosaur* Review • Week 7, Day 4 • Page 49 • Lesson Plan		
	Day 135			
Second Semester — Fourth Quarter				
Week 28	Day 136	*Noah's Ark Pre-School Activity Book* • (NAP) • N is for Noah • (DFD) • A is for Ark • Week 1, Day 1 • Page 51 • Lesson Plan		
	Day 137	B is for Back • Week 1, Day 2 • Page 51 • Lesson Plan		
	Day 138	C is for Called • Week 1, Day 3 • Page 51 • Lesson Plan		
	Day 139	D is for Dreadful • Week 1, Day 4 • Page 51 • Lesson Plan		
	Day 140			
Week 29	Day 141	E is for Earth • Week 2, Day 1 • Page 52 • Lesson Plan		
	Day 142	F is for Fruitful • Week 2, Day 2 • Page 52 • Lesson Plan		
	Day 143	G is for Grave • Week 2, Day 3 • Page 52 • Lesson Plan		
	Day 144	H is for Hear • Week 2, Day 4 • Page 52 • Lesson Plan		
	Day 145			
Week 30	Day 146	I is for Insane • Week 3, Day 1 • Page 53 • Lesson Plan		
	Day 147	J is for Judgment • Week 3, Day 2 • Page 53 • Lesson Plan		
	Day 148	K is for Kept • Week 3, Day 3 • Page 53 • Lesson Plan		
	Day 149	L is for Laughing • Week 3, Day 4 • Page 53 • Lesson Plan		
	Day 150			
Week 31	Day 151	M is for Mighty • Week 4, Day 1 • Page 54 • Lesson Plan		
	Day 152	N is for Noah • Week 4, Day 2 • Page 54 • Lesson Plan		
	Day 153	O is for Over • Week 4, Day 3 • Page 54 • Lesson Plan		
	Day 154	P is for Pleasure • Week 4, Day 4 • Page 54 • Lesson Plan		
	Day 155			
Week 32	Day 156	Q is for Quiet • Week 5, Day 1 • Page 55 • Lesson Plan		
	Day 157	R is for Raven • Week 5, Day 2 • Page 55 • Lesson Plan		
	Day 158	S is for Sent • Week 5, Day 3 • Page 55 • Lesson Plan		
	Day 159	T is for Twice • Week 5, Day 4 • Page 55 • Lesson Plan		
	Day 160			

Date	Day	Assignment	Due Date	✓
Week 33	Day 161	U is for Usher • Week 6, Day 1 • Page 56 • Lesson Plan		
	Day 162	V is for Very • Week 6, Day 2 • Page 56 • Lesson Plan		
	Day 163	W is for Wonderful • Week 6, Day 3 • Page 56• Lesson Plan		
	Day 164	X is in eXtensive • Week 6, Day 4 • Page 56 • Lesson Plan		
	Day 165			
Week 34	Day 166	Y is for Years • Week 7, Day 1 • Page 57 • Lesson Plan		
	Day 167	Z is for Zealous • Week 7, Day 2 • Page 57 • Lesson Plan		
	Day 168	*N is for Noah* Review • Week 7, Day 3 • Page 57 • Lesson Plan		
	Day 169	*N is for Noah* Review • Week 7, Day 4 • Page 57 • Lesson Plan		
	Day 170			
Week 35	Day 171	*Big Thoughts for Little Thinkers: The Scripture* • Week 1, Day 1 • Page 59 • Lesson Plan		
	Day 172	Big Thoughts • Week 1, Day 2 • Page 59 • Lesson Plan		
	Day 173	*Big Thoughts: The Gospel* • Week 1, Day 3 • Page 59 • Lesson Plan		
	Day 174	Big Thoughts • Week 1, Day 4 • Page 59 • Lesson Plan		
	Day 175			
Week 36	Day 176	*Big Thoughts: The Mission* • Week 2, Day 1 • Page 60 • Lesson Plan		
	Day 177	Big Thoughts • Week 2, Day 2 • Page 60 • Lesson Plan		
	Day 178	*Big Thoughts: The Trinity* • Week 2, Day 3 • Page 61 • Lesson Plan		
	Day 179	Big Thoughts • Week 2, Day 4 • Page 61• Lesson Plan		
	Day 180			

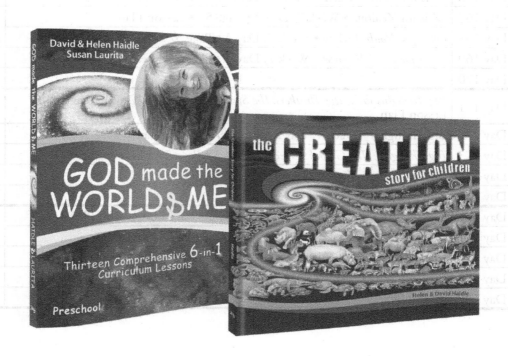

God made the World & Me

The Creation Story for Children

God Creates Light (*God Made the World and Me* pages 12 – 21)

Lesson 1, Day 1

I. CIRCLE TIME

Read Genesis 1:1–5 to your students.

- Talk about the concept of "empty," using activity 1 in the "Dear Parent" section on page 11.

- Talk about the concept of "dark" and "light," using activity 2 in the "Dear Parent" section on page 11.

Sing the "Circle Time Song" on page 16.

II. PHYSICAL CENTER

See page 13. If you have only one child, play the "Guess What I Am Thinking Of" game. The teacher should give a clue about the object he or she is thinking about that is located in the room. Clues can be about color, shape, size, etc. Let the students shine their flashlight on the object they think it is. If they are wrong, the teacher gives another clue. This continues until the student identifies the correct object.

Lesson 1, Day 2

I. CIRCLE TIME

Review Genesis 1:1–5

- Ask students to explain what Genesis 1:1–5 is about, filling in any parts they may have missed.

- Sing the "Circle Time Song" on page 16.

- Play the Night and Day Game on page 16.

- Introduce the Memory Verse on page 18.

II. SCIENCE CENTER

Complete option #1 on page 13.

Complete option #2 on page 14.

Note: Complete option on page 14 for older children.

Lesson 1, Day 3

I. CIRCLE TIME

- Sing the "Circle Time Song" on page 16.

- Read pages 2–5 of *Creation Story for Children*. Engage students in the Circle Time Discussion on page 17.

- Practice the Memory Verse on page 18.

II. ART CENTER

See page 15. Complete your choice of activities, based on whether you have older or younger students.

Lesson 1, Day 4

I. CIRCLE TIME

- Sing the "Circle Time Song" on page 16.

- Practice the Memory Verse on page 18.

II. REVIEW

- Color "God Creates Light" shown on page 20. Use student's copy in this PLP page 63.

- Complete Magazine COLOR Collage on page 21.

- Review Lesson 1 by completing the Closing on page 18. Give students a chance to recite their memory verse.

Lesson 2, Day 1
I. CIRCLE TIME
Read Genesis 1:6–8 to your students.

- Discuss the sky, using the discussion questions on page 19 in the "Next Time" section.

- Sing the "Circle Time Song" on page 26.

II. PHYSICAL CENTER
See page 23.

II. SCIENCE CENTER
See page 23. Begin creating graph of how the sky looks each day.

Lesson 2, Day 2
I. CIRCLE TIME
Review Genesis 1:6–8

- Ask students to explain what Genesis 1:6–8 is about, filling in any parts they may have missed.

- Sing the "Circle Time Song" on page 26.

- Introduce the Memory Verse on page 28.

II. SCIENCE CENTER
See page 23. Continue creating graph of how the sky looks each day.
Read a book or and/or look at pictures about weather or various skies. We suggest using Master Books' *Big Book of Earth & Sky.*

Lesson 2, Day 3
I. CIRCLE TIME

- Sing the "Circle Time Song" on page 26.

- Read pages 6–7 of *Creation Story for Children.* Engage students in the Circle Time Discussion on page 27.

- Practice the Memory Verse on page 28.

II. ART CENTER
Complete options #1 and #2 on pages 24–25. Note: Complete your choice of activities, based on whether you have older or younger students.

Lesson 2, Day 4
I. CIRCLE TIME

- Sing the "Circle Time Song" on page 26.

- Practice the Memory Verse on page 28.

II. SCIENCE CENTER
Complete Science Center activity and discussion questions on page 23.

III. REVIEW

- Color "God Creates the Sky" shown on page 30. Use student's copy in this PLP page 64.

- Complete "A Sky Full of AIR" on page 31.

- Learn "Finger Play — RAIN" on page 31.

- Review Lesson 2 by completing the Closing on page 28. Give students a chance to recite their memory verse.

God Creates Water (*God Made the World and Me* pages 32 – 41)

Lesson 3, Day 1
I. CIRCLE TIME
Read Genesis 1:9–10 to your students.

- Discuss the importance of water.

- Have students name all the ways they use water in a day.

Sing the "Circle Time Song" on page 36.

II. PHYSICAL CENTER
Complete option #1 and option #2 on page 33.

Lesson 3, Day 2
I. CIRCLE TIME
Review Genesis 1:9–10.

- Ask students to explain what Genesis 1:9–10 is about, filling in any parts they may have missed.

- Sing the "Circle Time Song" on page 36.

- Introduce the Memory Verse on page 38.

II. SCIENCE CENTER
See page 34.
Note: Complete your choice of activities, based on whether you have older or younger students.

Lesson 3, Day 3
I. CIRCLE TIME

- Sing the "Circle Time Song" on page 36.

- Read pages 8–9 of *Creation Story for Children*. Engage students in the Circle Time Discussion on page 37.

- Practice the Memory Verse on page 38.

II. ART CENTER
See page 35. Complete your choice of activities, based on whether you have older or younger students.

Lesson 3, Day 4
I. CIRCLE TIME

- Sing the "Circle Time Song" on page 36.

- Practice the Memory Verse on page 38.

II. REVIEW

- Color "God Creates Water" shown on page 40. Use student's copy in this PLP page 65.

- Complete "Bubble Fun" on page 41.

- Review Lesson 3 by completing the Closing on page 38. Give students a chance to recite their memory verse.

God Creates Land (*God Made the World and Me* pages 42 – 51)

Lesson 4, Day 1

I. CIRCLE TIME

Read Genesis 1:9–10 to your students.

- Discuss the many kinds of "land," including dirt, rocks, and sand.

- Help students find a pretty rock.

- Sing the "Circle Time Song" on page 46.

II. PHYSICAL CENTER

Complete option #1 and option #2 on page 43.

Lesson 4, Day 2

I. CIRCLE TIME

Review Genesis 1:9–10.

- Ask students to explain what Genesis 1:9–10 is about, filling in any parts they may have missed.

- Sing the "Circle Time Song" on page 46.

- Introduce the Memory Verse on page 48.

II. SCIENCE CENTER

See page 44.
Note: Complete your choice of activities, based on whether you have older or younger students.

Lesson 4, Day 3

I. CIRCLE TIME

- Sing the "Circle Time Song" on page 46.

- Review pages 8–9 of *Creation Story for Children*. Engage students in the Circle Time Discussion on page 47.

- Practice the Memory Verse on page 48.

II. ART CENTER

See page 45. See page 49 for final instructions for art center project.
Note: Complete your choice of activities, based on whether you have older or younger students.

Lesson 4, Day 4

I. CIRCLE TIME

- Sing the "Circle Time Song" on page 46.

- Practice the Memory Verse on page 48.

II. REVIEW

- Color "God Creates Land" shown on page 50. Use student's copy in this PLP page 66.

- Complete "Our FEET need LAND" on page 51.

- Review Lesson 4 by completing the Closing on page 48. Give students a chance to recite their memory verse.

God Creates Plants (*God Made the World and Me* pages 52 – 63)

Lesson 5, Day 1
I. CIRCLE TIME
Read Genesis 1:11–13 to your students.

- Discuss the many kinds of plants God made.

- Take a walk outside and see how many different kinds of plants you can find.

- Plan a field trip to visit a produce department or fruit stand this week. Try a new fruit or vegetable.

Sing the "Circle Time Song" on page 56.

II. PHYSICAL CENTER

- See page 53. You may adapt this activity for one student. Place all of the fruit and vegetables on a table. Have students run to the table and grab the kind of fruit or vegetable you call out. Have them place it in a bowl. Continue until all of the fruit and vegetables are in a bowl.

Lesson 5, Day 2
I. CIRCLE TIME
Review Genesis 1: 11–13.

- Ask students to explain what Genesis 1:11–13 is about, filling in any parts they may have missed.

- Sing the "Circle Time Song" on page 56.

- Introduce the Memory Verse on page 58.

II. SCIENCE CENTER
See pages 53–55. Complete options #1, #2, and #3.

Lesson 5, Day 3
I. CIRCLE TIME
Sing the "Circle Time Song" on page 56.

- Read pages 10–11 of *Creation Story for Children*. Engage students in the Circle Time Discussion on page 57.

- Practice the Memory Verse on page 58.

II. ART CENTER

- See page 54–55.

Note: Complete your choice of activities, based on whether you have older or younger students.

Lesson 5, Day 4
I. CIRCLE TIME

- Sing the "Circle Time Song" on page 56.

- Practice the Memory Verse on page 58.

II. REVIEW

- Color "God Creates Plants" shown on page 60. Use student's copy in this PLP page 67.

- Complete "Thank You, God, for Plants" on page 61.

- Complete "God Made Flowers" and "Play Dough Flowers" on page 62.

- Complete "Pin a Petal on the Flower" and "Sorting Flowers" on page 63.

- Review Lesson 5 by completing the Closing on page 58. Give students a chance to recite their memory verse.

God Creates Sun, Moon, Stars, & Planets (*God Made the World and Me* pages 64 – 73)

Lesson 6, Day 1

I. CIRCLE TIME

Read Genesis 1:16–18 to your students.

- Discuss the beauty of the sky, both day and night.

- Go outside and look up into the sky. See if you can find the moon in the daylight sky.

- Plan to spend 10–15 minutes looking up into the night sky.

- Sing the "Circle Time Song" on page 68.

II. PHYSICAL CENTER

See page 65. Complete Option #1 and Option #2. Note: Complete your choice of activities, based on whether you have older or younger students.

Lesson 6, Day 2

I. CIRCLE TIME

Review Genesis 1: 16–18.

- Ask students to explain what Genesis 1: 16–18 is about, filling in any parts they may have missed.

- Sing the "Circle Time Song" on page 68.

- Introduce the Memory Verse on page 70.

II. SCIENCE CENTER

See pages 65–66.

Lesson 6, Day 3

I. CIRCLE TIME

- Sing the "Circle Time Song" on page 68.

- Read pages 12–13 of *Creation Story for Children*. Engage students in the Circle Time Discussion on page 69.

- Practice the Memory Verse on page 70.

II. ART CENTER

See page 67.
Note: Complete your choice of activities, based on whether you have older or younger students.

Lesson 6, Day 4

I. CIRCLE TIME

- Sing the "Circle Time Song" on page 68.

- Practice the Memory Verse on page 70.

II. REVIEW

- Color "God Creates Sun & Stars" shown on page 72. Use student's copy in this PLP page 68.

- Complete "Make Hand Shadows" on page 73.

- Review Lesson 6 by completing the Closing on page 70. Give students a chance to recite their memory verse.

God Creates Sea Creatures (*God Made the World and Me* pages 74 – 87)

Lesson 7, Day 1

I. CIRCLE TIME

Read Genesis 1:20–22 to your students.

- Discuss the variety of God's sea creatures. Look at pictures in a book if you can.

- Plan to take a field trip to visit a local aquarium or pet store to see a variety of fish.

- Sing the "Circle Time Song" on page 78.

II. PHYSICAL CENTER

See page 76. If you only have one student, the instructor should move around like the creature and let the student guess.

Lesson 7, Day 2

I. CIRCLE TIME

Review Genesis 1: 20–22.

- •Ask students to explain what Genesis 1: 20–22 is about, filling in any parts they may have missed.

- Sing the "Circle Time Song" on page 78.

- Introduce the Memory Verse on page 80.

II. SCIENCE CENTER

See page 75.

Lesson 7, Day 3

I. CIRCLE TIME

- Sing the "Circle Time Song" on page 78.

- Read pages 14–15 of *Creation Story for Children*. Engage students in the Circle Time Discussion on page 79.

- Practice the Memory Verse on page 80.

II. ART CENTER

See pages 76–77.

Note: Complete your choice of activities, based on whether you have older or younger students.

Lesson 7, Day 4

I. CIRCLE TIME

- Sing the "Circle Time Song" on page 78.

- Practice the Memory Verse on page 80.

II. REVIEW

- Color "God Creates Sea Creatures" shown on page 82. Use student's copy in this PLP page 69.

- Complete "Five Red Crabs" shown on page 83. Use student's copy of the crab in this PLP page 70.

- Play "Guess Who I Am," using pages 84–87.

- Review Lesson 7 by completing the Closing on page 80. Give students a chance to recite their memory verse.

Lesson 8, Day 1

I. CIRCLE TIME

Read Genesis 1:20–22 to your students.

- Discuss the variety of God's birds. Look at pictures in a book if you can.

- Begin to track the number and kinds of birds around your house, as instructed on page 81 in the "Dear Parents" section.

- Sing the "Circle Time Song" on page 92.

II. PHYSICAL CENTER

See page 89. Complete Option #1 and Option #2.

Lesson 8, Day 2

I. CIRCLE TIME

Review Genesis 1: 20–22.

- Ask students to explain what Genesis 1: 20–22 is about, filling in any parts they may have missed.

- Sing the "Circle Time Song" on page 92.

- Introduce the Memory Verse on page 94.

II. SCIENCE CENTER

See page 90. Complete Option #1 and Option #2. Note: Complete your choice of activities based on whether you have older or younger students.

Lesson 8, Day 3

I. CIRCLE TIME

- Sing the "Circle Time Song" on page 92.

- Read pages 16–17 of *Creation Story for Children*. Engage students in the Circle Time Discussion on page 93.

- Practice the Memory Verse on page 94.

II. ART CENTER

See page 91. Complete Option #1 and Option #2. Note: Complete your choice of activities, based on whether you have older or younger students.

Lesson 8, Day 4

I. CIRCLE TIME

- Sing the "Circle Time Song" on page 92.

- Practice the Memory Verse on page 94.

II. REVIEW

- Color "God Creates BIRDS" shown on page 96. Use student's copy in this PLP page 71.

- Complete "Five Little Birds" shown on page 97. Use student's copy of the birds in this PLP page 72.

- Play "Guess Who I Am," using pages 98–99.

- Review Lesson 8 by completing the Closing on page 94. Give students a chance to recite their memory verse.

God Creates Animals (*God Made the World and Me* pages 100 – 115)

Lesson 9, Day 1

I. CIRCLE TIME

Read Genesis 1:24–25 to your students.

- Discuss the variety of God's animals. Use discussion question on page 95 in the "Dear Parents" section under "Read." Look at pictures in a book if you can.

- Work together to name one animal for every letter of the alphabet. (For "x" put the letter at the end of the word — fox.)

- Have your student find their favorite stuffed animal.

- Sing the "Circle Time Song" on page 104.

II. PHYSICAL CENTER

See page 101.

- Complete Option #1. To adapt this game for one student, help your student select stuffed animals or pictures of animals cut out of a magazine that represent a variety of animal kinds. When you call out different category of animals, let the student find a matching animal.

- Complete Option #2.

Lesson 9, Day 2

I. CIRCLE TIME

Review Genesis 1: 24–25.

- Ask students to explain what Genesis 1: 24–25 is about, filling in any parts they may have missed.

- Sing the "Circle Time Song" on page 104.

- Introduce the Memory Verse on page 106.

II. SCIENCE CENTER

See page 102.
Note: Complete your choice of activities, based on whether you have older or younger students.
God Creates Animals

Lesson 9, Day 3

I. CIRCLE TIME

- Sing the "Circle Time Song" on page 104.

- Read pages 18–19 of *Creation Story for Children*. Engage students in the Circle Time Discussion on page 105.

- Practice the Memory Verse on page 106.

II. ART CENTER

See page 103.

Lesson 9, Day 4

I. CIRCLE TIME

- Sing the "Circle Time Song" on page 104.

- Practice the Memory Verse on page 106.

II. REVIEW

- Color "God Creates Animals" shown on page 108. Use student's copy in this PLP page 73.

- Complete "Extra Game & Discussion" on page 109.

- Optional: "Extra Ideas for Projects and Study" on page 109.

- Play "Guess Who I Am" game on pages 110–115. For additional fun, mix up the type of animals and have students identify if the animal is a garden, farm, or zoo creature.

- Read pages 26–31 of *Creation Story for Children*. Discuss all of the amazing creatures God created.

- Review Lesson 9 by completing the Closing on page 106. Give students a chance to recite their memory verse.

God Creates People (*God Made the World and Me* pages 116 – 125)

Lesson 10, Day 1
I. CIRCLE TIME
Read Genesis 1:26–31 to your students.

- Discuss how people are made in the image of God and how this sets us apart from all of God's creation.

- Spend time with your student this week noticing the many wonderful things God designed about our bodies.

- Sing the "Circle Time Song" on page 120.

II. PHYSICAL CENTER
See page 117. Complete Option #1 and Option #2.

Lesson 10, Day 2
I. CIRCLE TIME
Review Genesis 1:26–31.

- Ask students to explain what Genesis 1:26–31 is about, filling in any parts they may have missed.

- Sing the "Circle Time Song" on page 120.

- Introduce the Memory Verse on page 122.

II. SCIENCE CENTER
See page 118. Adapt the Science Center for one student by having the student gather both boy and girl dolls and stuffed animals.
Note: Complete your choice of activities, based on whether you have older or younger students.

Lesson 10, Day 3
I. CIRCLE TIME

- Sing the "Circle Time Song" on page 120.

- Read pages 20–23 of *Creation Story for Children*. Engage students in the Circle Time Discussion on page 121.

- Practice the Memory Verse on page 122.

II. ART CENTER
See page 119.
Note: You can find the "picture of the globe with children's faces on page 36 of *Creation Story for Children*.
Note: Complete your choice of activities, based on whether you have older or younger students.

Lesson 10, Day 4
I. CIRCLE TIME

- Sing the "Circle Time Song" on page 120.

- Practice the Memory Verse on page 122.

II. REVIEW

- Color "God Creates People" shown on page 124. Use student's copy in this PLP page 74.

- Sing the song "God Made My Body" and act out the "Pantomime Poem" on page 125.

- Review Lesson 10 by completing the Closing on page 122. Give students a chance to recite their memory verse.

God Creates a Day of Rest (*God Made the World and Me* pages 126 – 135)

Lesson 11, Day 1

I. CIRCLE TIME

Read Genesis 2:1–3 to your students.

- Discuss the importance of rest.

- Plan some restful activities as suggested on page 123 in the "Dear Parents" section.

- Sing the "Circle Time Song" on page 130.

II. PHYSICAL CENTER

See page 127. Complete Option #1 and Option #2.

Lesson 11, Day 2

I. CIRCLE TIME

Review Genesis 2:1–3.

- Ask students to explain what Genesis 2:1–3 is about, filling in any parts they may have missed.

- Sing the "Circle Time Song" on page 130.

- Introduce the Memory Verse on page 132.

II. SCIENCE CENTER

See page 128.
Note: Complete your choice of activities, based on whether you have older or younger students.

Lesson 11, Day 3

I. CIRCLE TIME

- Sing the "Circle Time Song" on page 130.

- Read pages 24–25 of *Creation Story for Children*. Engage students in the Circle Time Discussion on page 131.

- Practice the Memory Verse on page 132.

II. ART CENTER

See page 129.
Note: Complete your choice of activities, based on whether you have older or younger students.

Lesson 11, Day 4

I. CIRCLE TIME

- Sing the "Circle Time Song" on page 130.

- Practice the Memory Verse on page 132.

II. REVIEW

- Color "God Creates a Day of Rest" shown on page 134. Use student's copy in this PLP page 75.

- Complete "Take Time for Creativity" and play "A Resting Game" on page 135.

- Review Lesson 11 by completing the Closing on page 132. Give students a chance to recite their memory verse.

Lesson 12, Day 1
I. CIRCLE TIME
Read Psalm 139:13–18 to your students.

- Discuss how God forms us inside our mothers' bodies.

- Discuss how God promises to never leave us, no matter what happens.

- Sing the "Circle Time Song" on page 140.

II. PHYSICAL CENTER
See page 137. Complete Option #1.
Complete Option #2. The game may be adapted to one student by having the instructor be the one to guess what kind of animal the student is acting out.

Lesson 12, Day 2
I. CIRCLE TIME
Review Psalm 139:13–18.

- Ask students to explain what Psalm 139:13–18 is about, filling in any parts they may have missed.

- Sing the "Circle Time Song" on page 140.

- Introduce the Memory Verse on page 142.

II. SCIENCE CENTER
See page 138.
Note: Complete your choice of activities, based on whether you have older or younger students.

Lesson 12, Day 3
I. CIRCLE TIME

- Sing the "Circle Time Song" on page 140.

- Read pages 32–36 of *Creation Story for Children*. Engage students in the Circle Time Discussion on page 141.

- Practice the Memory Verse on page 142.

II. ART CENTER
See page 139.
Note: Complete your choice of activities, based on whether you have older or younger students.

Lesson 12, Day 4
I. CIRCLE TIME

- Sing the "Circle Time Song" on page 140.

- Practice the Memory Verse on page 142.

II. REVIEW

- Color "God Created Me" shown on page 144. Use student's copy in this PLP page 76.

- Complete "God Made Me!" and read "Guess Who I Am" on page 145.

- Complete the Creation Mobile according to page 147. Use student's copy in this PLP pages 77 and 79.

- Review Lesson 12 by completing the Closing on page 142. Give students a chance to recite their memory verse.

Creation Celebration! (_God Made the World and Me_ pages 148 – 159)

Lesson 13, Day 1

I. CIRCLE TIME

Read Psalm 139:1–12 to your students.

- Discuss what Psalm 139 means to our lives.

- Give thanks for the gift of our life.

- Sing the "Circle Time Song" on page 152.

II. PHYSICAL CENTER

See page 149. Complete Option #1. For one student, use the final suggestion in this section. Complete Option #2. The game may be adapted to one student by having the instructor be the one to guess what kind of animal the student is acting out.

Lesson 13, Day 2

I. CIRCLE TIME

Review Psalm 139:1–12.

- Ask students to explain what Psalm 139:1–12 is about, filling in any parts they may have missed.

- Sing the "Circle Time Song" on page 152.

- Introduce the Memory Verse on page 154.

II. SCIENCE CENTER

See page 150.
Note: Complete your choice of activities, based on whether you have older or younger students.

Lesson 13, Day 3

I. CIRCLE TIME

- Sing the "Circle Time Song" on page 152.

- Hold up pages 22–23 of _Creation Story for Children_. Engage students in the Circle Time Discussion on page 153.

- Practice the Memory Verse on page 154.

II. ART CENTER

See page 151.
Note: Complete your choice of activities, based on whether you have older or younger students.

Lesson 13, Day 4

I. CIRCLE TIME

- Sing the "Circle Time Song" on page 152.

- Practice the Memory Verse on page 154.

II. REVIEW

- Color "Celebrate Creation" shown on page 156. Use student's copy in this PLP page 81.

- Use Ideas for Learning Centers on page 157.

- Play "Guess Who I Am" on pages 158–159.

- Review Lesson 12 by completing the Closing on page 154. Give students a chance to recite their memory verse.

A Is for Adam (*A is for Adam* pages 1-8 and Notes page 53-57)

Week 1, Day 1

I. CIRCLE TIME

Read the *A Is for Adam* book pages 2–52.
Re-read "A is for Adam" on page 2. Complete page 1 sections:

- The Starting Point

- Bible Bits

- Let's Talk

- Always Remember

II. STUFF TO DO

Complete "A is for Adam" coloring sheet. Use student's copy in this PLP on page 82. See page 1 for Stuff to Do. Plan a trip to the zoo.

III. QUICK REVIEW

See page 1. Go deeper for older students on page 53.

Week 1, Day 2

I. CIRCLE TIME

Read "B is for Bible" on page 4. Complete page 3 sections:

- The Starting Point

- Bible Bits

- Let's Talk

- Always Remember

- Visual Vocabulary

II. STUFF TO DO

Complete "B is for Bible" coloring Sheet. Use student's copy in this PLP on page 83. See page 3 for Stuff to Do. Complete Chart. Use chart of page 84 of this PLP.

III. QUICK REVIEW

See page 3. Go deeper for older students on pages 54–55.

Week 1, Day 3

I. CIRCLE TIME

Read "C is for Creatures" on page 6. Complete page 5 sections:

- The Starting Point

- Bible Bits

- Let's Talk

- Always Remember

- Visual Vocabulary

II. EXTRA ACTIVITIES

Complete "C is for Creatures" coloring sheet. Use student's copy in this PLP page 85. See page 5 for Extra Activities.

III. QUICK REVIEW

See page 5. Go deeper for older students on page 55–56.

Week 1, Day 4

I. CIRCLE TIME

Read "D is for Dinosaur" on page 8. Complete page 7 sections:

- The Starting Point

- Bible Bits

- Let's Talk

- Always Remember

- Visual Vocabulary

II. STUFF TO DO

Complete "D is for Dinosaur" coloring sheet. Use student's copy in this PLP page 86. See page 7 for Stuff to Do.

III. QUICK REVIEW

See page 7. Go deeper for older students on page 57.

Week 2, Day 1
I. CIRCLE TIME
Read "E is for Eve" on page 10. Complete page 9 sections:

- The Starting Point

- Bible Bits

- Let's Talk

- Always Remember

- Visual Vocabulary

II. STUFF TO DO
Complete "E is for Eve" coloring sheet. Use student's copy in this PLP page 87. See page 9 for Stuff to Do.

III. QUICK REVIEW
See page 9. Go deeper for older students on page 58.

Week 2, Day 2
I. CIRCLE TIME
Read "F is for Fruit" on page 12. Complete page 11 sections:

- The Starting Point

- Bible Bits

- Let's Talk

- Always Remember

- Visual Vocabulary

II. STUFF TO DO
Complete "F is for Fruit" coloring sheet. Use student's copy in this PLP page 88. See page 11 for Stuff to Do.

III. QUICK REVIEW
See page 11. Go deeper for older students on page 60.

Week 2, Day 3
I. CIRCLE TIME
Read "G is for Ghastly" on page 14. Complete page 13 sections:

- The Starting Point

- Bible Bits

- Let's Talk

- Always Remember

- Visual Vocabulary

II. STUFF TO DO
Complete "G is for Ghastly" coloring sheet. Use student's copy in this PLP page 89.
See page 13 for Stuff to Do. Plan a walk or drive through several streets to find things we are supposed to obey.

III. QUICK REVIEW
See page 13. Go deeper for older students on page 61.

Week 2, Day 4
I. CIRCLE TIME
Read "H is for How" on page 16. Complete page 15 sections:

- The Starting Point

- Bible Bits

- Let's Talk

- Always Remember

- Visual Vocabulary

II. EXTRA ACTIVITIES
Complete "H is for How" coloring sheet. Use student's copy in this PLP page 90. See page 15 for Stuff to Do.

III. QUICK REVIEW
See page 15. Go deeper for older students on page 62.

Week 3, Day 1
I. CIRCLE TIME
Read "I is for Interested" on page 18. Complete page 17 sections:

- The Starting Point

- Bible Bits

- Let's Talk

- Always Remember

II. STUFF TO DO
Complete "I is for Interested" coloring sheet. Use student's copy in this PLP page 91. See page 17 for Stuff to Do.

III. QUICK REVIEW
See page 17. Go deeper for older students on page 63.

Week 3, Day 2
I. CIRCLE TIME
Read "J is for Jovial" on page 20. Complete page 19 sections:

- The Starting Point

- Bible Bits

- Let's Talk

- Always Remember

II. STUFF TO DO
Complete "J is for Jovial" coloring sheet. Use student's copy in this PLP page 92. See page 19 for Stuff to Do.

III. QUICK REVIEW
See page 19. Go deeper for older students on page 64.

Week 3, Day 3
I. CIRCLE TIME
Read "K is for Knew" on page 22. (Explain to students that the "K" is silent in Knew.)
Complete page 21 sections:

- The Starting Point

- Bible Bits

- Let's Talk

- Always Remember

II. STUFF TO DO
Complete "K is for Knew" coloring sheet. Use student's copy in this PLP page 93. See page 21 for Stuff to Do. Plan a walk or drive through several streets to find things we are supposed to obey.

III. QUICK REVIEW
See page 21. Go deeper for older students on page 66.

Week 3, Day 4
I. CIRCLE TIME
Read "L is for Lord" on page 24. Complete page 23 sections:

- The Starting Point

- Bible Bits

- Let's Talk

- Always Remember

- Visual Vocabulary

II. EXTRA ACTIVITIES
Complete "L is for Lord" coloring sheet. Use student's copy in this PLP page 94. See page 23 for Stuff to Do. (If you do not have a rosebush in your yard, find pictures that show the thorns as well as the flower.)

III. QUICK REVIEW
See page 23. Go deeper for older students on page 67.

Week 4, Day 1
I. CIRCLE TIME
Read "M is for Moan" on page 26. Complete page 25 sections:

- The Starting Point

- Bible Bits

- Let's Talk

- Always Remember

II. STUFF TO DO
Complete "M is for Moan" coloring sheet. Use student's copy in this PLP page 95. See page 25 for Stuff to Do.

III. QUICK REVIEW
See page 25. Go deeper for older students on page 68.

Week 4, Day 2
I. CIRCLE TIME
Read "N is for Never" on page 28. Complete page 27 sections:

- The Starting Point

- Bible Bits

- Let's Talk

- Always Remember

II. STUFF TO DO
Complete "N is for Never" coloring sheet. Use student's copy in this PLP page 96. See page 27 for Stuff to Do.

III. QUICK REVIEW
See page 27. Go deeper for older students on page 69.

Week 4, Day 3
I. CIRCLE TIME
Read "O is for Offering" on page 30. Complete page 29 sections:

- The Starting Point

- Bible Bits

- Let's Talk

- Always Remember

II. STUFF TO DO
Complete "O is for Offering" coloring sheet. Use student's copy in this PLP page 97. See page 29 for Stuff to Do.

III. QUICK REVIEW
See page 29. Go deeper for older students on page 69.

Week 4, Day 4
I. CIRCLE TIME
Read "P is for Plan" on page 32. Complete page 31 sections:

- The Starting Point

- Bible Bits

- Let's Talk

- Always Remember

II. EXTRA ACTIVITIES
Complete "P is for Plan" coloring sheet. Use student's copy in this PLP page 98. See page 31 for Extra Activities.

III. QUICK REVIEW
See page 31. Go deeper for older students on page 71.

A Is for Adam (*A is for Adam* pages 33-40 and Notes page 71-74)

Week 5, Day 1

I. CIRCLE TIME

Read "Q is for Quiet" on page 34. Complete page 33 sections:

- The Starting Point

- Bible Bits

- Let's Talk

- Always Remember

II. STUFF TO DO

Complete "Q is for Quiet" coloring sheet. Use student's copy in this PLP page 99. See page 33 for Stuff to Do, Use student's copy in this PLP page 101.

III. QUICK REVIEW

See page 33. Go deeper for older students on page 71.

Week 5, Day 2

I. CIRCLE TIME

Read "R is for Rough" on page 36. Complete page 35 sections:

- The Starting Point

- Bible Bits

- Let's Talk

- Always Remember

- Visual Vocabulary

II. STUFF TO DO

Complete "R is for Rough" coloring sheet. Use student's copy in this PLP page 100. See page 35 for Stuff to Do.

III. QUICK REVIEW

See page 35. Go deeper for older students on page 72.

Week 5, Day 3

I. CIRCLE TIME

Read "S is for Seventy" on page 38. Complete page 37 sections:

- The Starting Point

- Bible Bits

- Let's Talk

- Always Remember

- Visual Vocabulary

II. STUFF TO DO

Complete "S is for Seventy" coloring sheet. Use student's copy in this PLP page 103. See page 37 for Stuff to Do.

III. QUICK REVIEW

See page 37. Go deeper for older students on page 73.

Week 5, Day 4

I. CIRCLE TIME

Read "T is for Trouble" on page 40. Complete page 39 sections:

- The Starting Point

- Bible Bits

- Let's Talk

- Always Remember

- Visual Vocabulary

II. EXTRA ACTIVITIES

Complete "T is for Trouble" coloring sheet. Use student's copy in this PLP page 104. See page 39 for Extra Activities.

III. QUICK REVIEW

See page 39. Go deeper for older students on page 74.

Week 6, Day 1
I. CIRCLE TIME
Read "U is for Utterly" on page 42. Complete page 41 sections:

- The Starting Point

- Bible Bits

- Let's Talk

- Always Remember

II. STUFF TO DO
Complete "U is for Utterly" coloring sheet. Use student's copy in this PLP page 105. See page 41 for Stuff to Do.

III. QUICK REVIEW
See page 41. Go deeper for older students on page 74.

Week 6, Day 2
I. CIRCLE TIME
Read "V is for Violent" on page 44. Complete page 43 sections:

- The Starting Point

- Bible Bits

- Let's Talk

- Always Remember

II. STUFF TO DO
Complete "V is for Violent" coloring sheet. Use student's copy in this PLP page 106. See page 43 for Stuff to Do.

III. QUICK REVIEW
See page 43. Go deeper for older students on page 75.

Week 6, Day 3
I. CIRCLE TIME
Read "W is for Walk" on page 46. Complete page 45 sections:

- The Starting Point

- Bible Bits

- Let's Talk

- Always Remember

II. STUFF TO DO
Complete "W is for Walk" coloring sheet. Use student's copy in this PLP page 107. See page 45 for Stuff to Do.

III. QUICK REVIEW
See page 45. Go deeper for older students on page 76.

Week 6, Day 4
I. CIRCLE TIME
Read "X is for Explode" on page 48. (Explain to children that the letter "x" is in the middle of Explode.) Complete page 47 sections:

- The Starting Point

- Bible Bits

- Let's Talk

- Always Remember

II. EXTRA ACTIVITIES
Complete "X is for Explode" coloring sheet. Use student's copy in this PLP page 108. See page 47 for Stuff to Do.

III. QUICK REVIEW
See page 47. Go deeper for older students on page 76.

A Is for Adam (*A is for Adam* pages 50-52 and Notes page 76-77)

Week 7, Day 1
I. CIRCLE TIME
Read "Y is for Yes" on page 50. Complete page 49 sections:

- The Starting Point

- Bible Bits

- Let's Talk

- Always Remember

II. STUFF TO DO
Complete "Y is for Yes" coloring sheet. Use student's copy in this PLP page 109. See page 49 for Stuff to Do.

III. QUICK REVIEW
See page 49. Go deeper for older students on page 76.

Week 7, Day 2
I. CIRCLE TIME
Read "Z is for Zip" on page 52. Complete page 51 sections:

- The Starting Point

- Bible Bits

- Let's Talk

- Always Remember

II. STUFF TO DO
Complete "Z is for Zip" coloring sheet. Use student's copy in this PLP page 110. See page 51 for Stuff to Do.

III. QUICK REVIEW
See page 51. Go deeper for older students on page 77.

Week 7, Day 3
I. CIRCLE TIME
Read *A is for Adam* pages 2–52.
Work with student to memorize what each letter of the alphabet in *A is for Adam* stands for. The instructor should say the name of the letter and let the student say what it stands for. Older students may be able say both the letter and what it stands for while going through the alphabet.

Week 7, Day 4
I. CIRCLE TIME
Read *A is for Adam* pages 2–52.
Continue to work with the student to memorize what each letter of the alphabet in *A is for Adam* stands for. The instructor should say the name of the letter and let the student say what it stands for. Older students may be able say both the letter and what it stands for while going through the alphabet.
Watch the *A is for Adam* DVD as a reward for a job well done.

D Is for Dinosaur (*D is for Dinosaur* pages 1-8 and Notes page 53-56)

Week 1, Day 1

I. CIRCLE TIME

Read the *D is for Dinosaur* book pages 2–52. Re-read "A is for Answers" on page 2. Complete page 1 sections:

- The Starting Point

- Bible Bits

- Let's Talk

- Always Remember

II. STUFF TO DO

Complete "A is for Answers" coloring sheet. Use student's copy in this PLP page 111. See page 1 for Stuff to Do.

III. QUICK REVIEW

See page 1. Go deeper for older students on page 53.

Week 1, Day 2

I. CIRCLE TIME

Read "B is for Bible" on page 4. Complete page 3 sections:

- The Starting Point

- Bible Bits

- Let's Talk

- Always Remember

II. STUFF TO DO

Complete "B is for Bible" coloring Sheet. Use student's copy in this PLP page 112. See page 3 for Stuff to Do.

III. QUICK REVIEW

See page 3. Go deeper for older students on page 54.

Week 1, Day 3

I. CIRCLE TIME

Read "C is for Continent" on page 6. Complete page 5 sections:

- The Starting Point

- Bible Bits

- Let's Talk

- Always Remember

II. STUFF TO DO

Complete "C is for Continent" coloring sheet. Use student's copy in this PLP page 113. See page 5 for Stuff to Do.

III. QUICK REVIEW

See page 5. Go deeper for older students on page 55.

Week 1, Day 4

I. CIRCLE TIME

Read "D is for Dinosaur" on page 8. Complete page 7 sections:

- The Starting Point

- Bible Bits

- Let's Talk

- Always Remember

II. STUFF TO DO

Complete "D is for Dinosaur" coloring sheet. Use student's copy in this PLP page 114. See page 7 for Stuff to Do.

III. QUICK REVIEW

See page 7. Go deeper for older students on page 56.

Week 2, Day 1
I. CIRCLE TIME
Read "E is for Everything" on page 10. Complete page 9 sections:

- The Starting Point

- Bible Bits

- Let's Talk

- Always Remember

II. STUFF TO DO
Complete "E is for Everything" coloring sheet. Use student's copy in this PLP page 115. See page 9 for Stuff to Do.

III. QUICK REVIEW
See page 9. Go deeper for older students on page 57.

Week 2, Day 2
I. CIRCLE TIME
Read "F is for Fantastic" on page 12. Complete page 11 sections:

- The Starting Point

- Bible Bits

- Let's Talk

- Always Remember

II. STUFF TO DO
Complete "F is for Fantastic" coloring sheet. Use student's copy in this PLP page 116. See page 11 for Stuff to Do.

III. QUICK REVIEW
See page 11. Go deeper for older students on page 57.

Week 2, Day 3
I. CIRCLE TIME
Read "G is for Garden" on page 14. Complete page 13 sections:

- The Starting Point

- Bible Bits

- Let's Talk

- Always Remember

II. STUFF TO DO
Complete "G is for Garden" coloring sheet. Use student's copy in this PLP page 117. See page 13 for Stuff to Do. Plan a walk outside in a garden or a park.

III. QUICK REVIEW
See page 13. Go deeper for older students on page 58.

Week 2, Day 4
I. CIRCLE TIME
Read "H is for Hungry" on page 16. Complete page 15 sections:

- The Starting Point

- Bible Bits

- Let's Talk

- Always Remember

II. STUFF TO DO
Complete "H is for Hungry" coloring sheet. Use student's copy in this PLP page 118. See page 15 for Stuff to Do. Plan a visit to your kitchen or a grocery store.

III. QUICK REVIEW
See page 15. Go deeper for older students on page 58.

Week 3, Day 1

I. CIRCLE TIME

Read "I is the letter in the middle of Sin" on page 18. Complete page 17 sections:

- The Starting Point

- Bible Bits

- Let's Talk

- Always Remember

II. STUFF TO DO

Complete "I in the middle Sin" coloring sheet. Use student's copy in this PLP page 119. See page 17 for Stuff to Do.

III. QUICK REVIEW

See page 17. Go deeper for older students on page 59.

Week 3, Day 2

I. CIRCLE TIME

Read "J means Just awful" on page 20. Complete page 19 sections:

- The Starting Point

- Bible Bits

- Let's Talk

- Always Remember

II. STUFF TO DO

Complete "J means Just awful" coloring sheet. Use student's copy in this PLP page 120. See page 19 for Stuff to Do.

III. QUICK REVIEW

See page 19. Go deeper for older students on page 60.

Week 3, Day 3

I. CIRCLE TIME

Read "K is for Knowledge" on page 22. (Explain to students that the "K" is silent in Knowledge.) Complete page 21 sections:

- The Starting Point

- Bible Bits

- Let's Talk

- Always Remember

II. STUFF TO DO

Complete "K is for Knowledge" coloring sheet. Use student's copy in this PLP page 121. See page 21 for Stuff to Do.

III. QUICK REVIEW

See page 21. Go deeper for older students on page 60.

Week 3, Day 4

I. CIRCLE TIME

Read "L is for Listen" on page 24. Complete page 23 sections:

- The Starting Point

- Bible Bits

- Let's Talk

- Always Remember

II. STUFF TO DO

Complete "L is for Listen" coloring sheet. Use student's copy in this PLP page 122. See page 23 for Stuff to Do.

III. QUICK REVIEW

See page 23. Go deeper for older students on page 61.

Week 4, Day 1
I. CIRCLE TIME
Read "M is for Monster" on page 26. Complete page 25 sections:

- The Starting Point

- Bible Bits

- Let's Talk

- Always Remember

II. STUFF TO DO
Complete "M is for Monster" coloring sheet. Use student's copy in this PLP page 123. See page 25 for Stuff to Do.

III. QUICK REVIEW
See page 25. Go deeper for older students on page 62.

Week 4, Day 2
I. CIRCLE TIME
Read "N is for Noah" on page 28. Complete page 27 sections:

- The Starting Point

- Bible Bits

- Let's Talk

- Always Remember

II. STUFF TO DO
Complete "N is for Noah" coloring sheet. Use student's copy in this PLP page 124. See page 27 for Stuff to Do.

III. QUICK REVIEW
See page 27. Go deeper for older students on page 63.

Week 4, Day 3
I. CIRCLE TIME
Read "O is for Out" on page 30. Complete page 29 sections:

- The Starting Point

- Bible Bits

- Let's Talk

- Always Remember

II. STUFF TO DO
Complete "O is for Out" coloring sheet. Use student's copy in this PLP page 125. See page 29 for Stuff to Do. Use *Dinosaurs By Design* to see different kinds of dinosaurs.

III. QUICK REVIEW
See page 29. Go deeper for older students on page 63.

Week 4, Day 4
I. CIRCLE TIME
Read "P is for Pronounce" on page 32. Complete page 31 sections:

- The Starting Point

- Bible Bits

- Let's Talk

- Always Remember

II. STUFF TO DO
Complete "P is for Pronounce" coloring sheet. Use student's copy in this PLP page 126. See page 31 for Stuff to Do. Use *Dinosaurs By Design*.

III. QUICK REVIEW
See page 31. Go deeper for older students on page 64.

Week 5, Day 1

I. CIRCLE TIME

Read "Q is for Question" on page 34. Complete page 33 sections:

- The Starting Point

- Bible Bits

- Let's Talk

- Always Remember

II. STUFF TO DO

Complete "Q is for Question" coloring sheet. Use student's copy in this PLP page 127. See page 33 for Stuff to Do.

III. QUICK REVIEW

See page 33. Go deeper for older students on page 64.

Week 5, Day 2

I. CIRCLE TIME

Read "R is for Reasons" on page 36. Complete page 35 sections:

- The Starting Point

- Bible Bits

- Let's Talk

- Always Remember

II. STUFF TO DO

Complete "R is for Reasons" coloring sheet. Use student's copy in this PLP page 128. See page 35 for Stuff to Do.

III. QUICK REVIEW

See page 35. Go deeper for older students on page 65.

Week 5, Day 3

I. CIRCLE TIME

Read "S is for Section" on page 38. Complete page 37 sections:

- The Starting Point

- Bible Bits

- Let's Talk

- Always Remember

II. STUFF TO DO

Complete "S is for Section" coloring sheet. Use student's copy in this PLP page 129. See page 37 for Stuff to Do.

III. QUICK REVIEW

See page 37. Go deeper for older students on page 66.

Week 5, Day 4

I. CIRCLE TIME

Read "T is for Tales" on page 40. Complete page 39 sections:

- The Starting Point

- Bible Bits

- Let's Talk

- Always Remember

II. STUFF TO DO

Complete "T is for Tales" coloring sheet. Use student's copy in this PLP page 130. Read *When Dragon Hearts Were Good*. See page 39 for Stuff to Do.

III. QUICK REVIEW

See page 39. Go deeper for older students on page 67.

Week 6, Day 1

I. CIRCLE TIME

Read "U is for Understand" on page 42. Complete page 41 sections:

- The Starting Point

- Bible Bits

- Let's Talk

- Always Remember

II. STUFF TO DO

Complete "U is for Understand" coloring sheet. Use student's copy in this PLP page 131. See page 41 for Stuff to Do. Plan a trip to your bookshelf or the library.

III. QUICK REVIEW

See page 41. Go deeper for older students on page 68.

Week 6, Day 2

I. CIRCLE TIME

Read "V is for how Very much" on page 44. Complete page 43 sections:

- The Starting Point

- Bible Bits

- Let's Talk

- Always Remember

II. STUFF TO DO

Complete "V is for how Very much" coloring sheet. Use student's copy in this PLP page 132. See page 43 for Stuff to Do.

III. QUICK REVIEW

See page 43. Go deeper for older students on page 68.

Week 6, Day 3

I. CIRCLE TIME

Read "W is for Watchfulness" on page 46. Complete page 45 sections:

- The Starting Point

- Bible Bits

- Let's Talk

- Always Remember

II. STUFF TO DO

Complete "W is for Watchfulness" coloring sheet. Use student's copy in this PLP page 133. See page 45 for Stuff to Do.

III. QUICK REVIEW

See page 45. Go deeper for older students on page 69.

Week 6, Day 4

I. CIRCLE TIME

Read "X is in eXcited" on page 48. (Explain to children that the letter "x" is in the middle of Excited.) Complete page 47 sections:

- The Starting Point

- Bible Bits

- Let's Talk

- Always Remember

II. STUFF TO DO

Complete "X is in eXcited" coloring sheet. Use student's copy in this PLP page 134. See page 47 for Stuff to Do.

III. QUICK REVIEW

See page 47. Go deeper for older students on page 70.

Week 7, Day 1
I. CIRCLE TIME
Read "Y is for Years" on page 50. Complete page 49 sections:

- The Starting Point

- Bible Bits

- Let's Talk

- Always Remember

II. STUFF TO DO
Complete "Y is for Years" coloring sheet. Use student's copy in this PLP page 135. See page 49 for Stuff to Do.

III. QUICK REVIEW
See page 49. Go deeper for older students on page 70.

Week 7, Day 2
I. CIRCLE TIME
Read "Z is for Zeal" on page 52. Complete page 51 sections:

- The Starting Point

- Bible Bits

- Let's Talk

- Always Remember

II. STUFF TO DO
Complete "Z is for Zeal" coloring sheet. Use student's copy in this PLP page 136. See page 51 for Stuff to Do.

III. QUICK REVIEW
See page 51. Go deeper for older students on page 71.

Week 7, Day 3
I. CIRCLE TIME
Read *D is for Dinosaur* pages 2–52.
Work with student to memorize what each letter of the alphabet in *D is for Dinosaur* stands for. The instructor should say the name of the letter and let the student say what it stands for. Older students may be able say both the letter and what it stands for while going through the alphabet.
Read *Dinosaurs: Stars of the Show.*

Week 7, Day 4
I. CIRCLE TIME
Read *D is for Dinosaur* pages 2–52.
Continue to work with the student to memorize what each letter of the alphabet in D is for Dinosaur stands for. The instructor should say the name of the letter and let the student say what it stands for. Older students may be able say both the letter and what it stands for while going through the alphabet.
Watch the *D is for Dinosaur* DVD as a reward for a job well done.

N is for Noah (*N is for Noah* pages 1-8 and Notes pages 53-55)

Week 1, Day 1

I. CIRCLE TIME

Read the *N is for Noah* book pages 2–52. Re-read "A is for Ark" on page 2. Complete page 1 sections:

- The Starting Point
- Bible Bits
- Let's Talk
- Always Remember

II. STUFF TO DO

Complete "A is for Ark" coloring sheet. Use student's copy in this PLP page 138. See page 1 for Stuff to Do.

III. QUICK REVIEW

See page 1. Go deeper for older students on page 53.

IV. NOAH'S ARK PRE-SCHOOL ACTIVITY BOOK

Optional: Complete pages 3–5. Parents should read each page to students.

Week 1, Day 2

I. CIRCLE TIME

Read "B is for Back" on page 4. Complete page 3 sections:

- The Starting Point
- Bible Bits
- Let's Talk
- Always Remember

II. STUFF TO DO

Complete "B is for Back" coloring Sheet. Use student's copy in this PLP page 139. See page 3 for Stuff to Do.

III. QUICK REVIEW

See page 3. Go deeper for older students on page 53.

IV. NOAH'S ARK PRE-SCHOOL ACTIVITY BOOK

Complete pages 6–7. Parents should read each page to students.

Week 1, Day 3

I. CIRCLE TIME

Read "C is for Called" on page 6. Complete page 5 sections:

- The Starting Point
- Bible Bits
- Let's Talk
- Always Remember

II. STUFF TO DO

Complete "C is for Called" coloring sheet. Use student's copy in this PLP page 140. See page 5 for Stuff to Do.

III. QUICK REVIEW

See page 5. Go deeper for older students on page 54.

IV. NOAH'S ARK PRE-SCHOOL ACTIVITY BOOK

Complete pages 8–9. Parents should read each page to students.

Week 1, Day 4

I. CIRCLE TIME

Read "D is for Dreadful" on page 8. Complete page 7 sections:

- The Starting Point
- Bible Bits
- Let's Talk
- Always Remember

II. STUFF TO DO

Complete "D is for Dreadful" coloring sheet. Use student's copy in this PLP page 141. See page 7 for Stuff to Do.

III. QUICK REVIEW

See page 7. Go deeper for older students on page 55.

IV. NOAH'S ARK PRE-SCHOOL ACTIVITY BOOK

Complete pages 10–11. Parents should read each page to students.

Week 2, Day 1
I. CIRCLE TIME
Read "E is for Earth" on page 10. Complete page 9 sections:

- The Starting Point
- Bible Bits
- Let's Talk
- Always Remember

II. STUFF TO DO
Complete "E is for Earth" coloring sheet. Use student's copy in this PLP page 142. See page 9 for Stuff to Do.

III. QUICK REVIEW
See page 9. Go deeper for older students on page 56.

IV. NOAH'S ARK PRE-SCHOOL ACTIVITY BOOK
Complete pages 12–13. Parents should read each page to students.

Week 2, Day 2
I. CIRCLE TIME
Read "F is for Fruitful" on page 12. Complete page 11 sections:

- The Starting Point
- Bible Bits
- Let's Talk
- Always Remember

II. STUFF TO DO
Complete "F is for Fruitful" coloring sheet. Use student's copy in this PLP page 143. See page 11 for Stuff to Do.

III. QUICK REVIEW
See page 11. Go deeper for older students on page 57.

IV. NOAH'S ARK PRE-SCHOOL ACTIVITY BOOK
Complete pages 14–15. Parents should read each page to students.

Week 2, Day 3
I. CIRCLE TIME
Read "G is for Grave" on page 14. Complete page 13 sections:

- The Starting Point
- Bible Bits
- Let's Talk
- Always Remember

II. STUFF TO DO
Complete G is for Grave coloring sheet. Use student's copy in this PLP page 144. See page 13 for Stuff to Do.

III. QUICK REVIEW
See page 13. Go deeper for older students on page 58.

IV. NOAH'S ARK PRE-SCHOOL ACTIVITY BOOK
Complete pages 16–18. Parents should read each page to students.

Week 2, Day 4
I. CIRCLE TIME
Read "H is for Hear" on page 16. Complete page 15 sections:

- The Starting Point
- Bible Bits
- Let's Talk
- Always Remember

II. STUFF TO DO
Complete "H is for Hear" coloring sheet. Use student's copy in this PLP page 145. See page 15 for Stuff to Do.

III. QUICK REVIEW
See page 15. Go deeper for older students on page 58.

IV. NOAH'S ARK PRE-SCHOOL ACTIVITY BOOK
Complete pages 19–21. Parents should read each page to students.

Week 3, Day 1

I. CIRCLE TIME

Read "I is for Insane" on page 18. Complete page 17 sections:

- The Starting Point
- Bible Bits
- Let's Talk
- Always Remember

II. STUFF TO DO

Complete "I is for Insane" coloring sheet. Use student's copy in this PLP page 146. See page 17 for Stuff to Do.

III. QUICK REVIEW

See page 17. Go deeper for older students on page 59.

IV. NOAH'S ARK PRE-SCHOOL ACTIVITY BOOK

Complete pages 22–23. Parents should read each page to students.

Week 3, Day 2

I. CIRCLE TIME

Read "J is for Judgment" on page 20. Complete page 19 sections:

- The Starting Point
- Bible Bits
- Let's Talk
- Always Remember

II. STUFF TO DO

Complete "J is for Judgment" coloring sheet. Use student's copy in this PLP page 147. See page 19 for Stuff to Do. Visit a park or large yard.

III. QUICK REVIEW

See page 19. Go deeper for older students on page 59.

IV. NOAH'S ARK PRE-SCHOOL ACTIVITY BOOK

Complete pages 24–25. Parents should read each page to students

Week 3, Day 3

I. CIRCLE TIME

Read "K is for Kept" on page 22. Complete page 21 sections:

- The Starting Point
- Bible Bits
- Let's Talk
- Always Remember

II. STUFF TO DO

Complete "K is for Kept" coloring sheet. Use student's copy in this PLP page 148. See page 21 for Stuff to Do.

III. QUICK REVIEW

See page 21. Go deeper for older students on page 60.

IV. NOAH'S ARK PRE-SCHOOL ACTIVITY BOOK

Complete pages 26–27. Parents should read each page to students.

Week 3, Day 4

I. CIRCLE TIME

Read "L is for Laughing" on page 24. Complete page 23 sections:

- The Starting Point
- Bible Bits
- Let's Talk
- Always Remember

II. STUFF TO DO

Complete "L is for Laughing" coloring sheet. Use student's copy in this PLP page 149. See page 23 for Stuff to Do.

III. QUICK REVIEW

See page 23. Go deeper for older students on page 61.

IV. NOAH'S ARK PRE-SCHOOL ACTIVITY BOOK

Complete pages 28–29. Parents should read each page to students.

Week 4, Day 1

I. CIRCLE TIME

Read "M is for Mighty" on page 26. Complete page 25 sections:

- The Starting Point
- Bible Bits
- Let's Talk
- Always Remember

II. STUFF TO DO

Complete "M is for Mighty" coloring sheet. Use student's copy in this PLP page 150. See page 25 for Stuff to Do.

III. QUICK REVIEW

See page 25. Go deeper for older students on page 61.

IV. NOAH'S ARK PRE-SCHOOL ACTIVITY BOOK

Complete pages 30–31. Parents should read each page to students.

Week 4, Day 2

I. CIRCLE TIME

Read "N is for Noah" on page 28. Complete page 27 sections:

- The Starting Point
- Bible Bits
- Let's Talk
- Always Remember

II. STUFF TO DO

Complete "N is for Noah" coloring sheet. Use student's copy in this PLP page 151. See page 27 for Stuff to Do.

III. QUICK REVIEW

See page 27. Go deeper for older students on page 62.

IV. NOAH'S ARK PRE-SCHOOL ACTIVITY BOOK

Complete pages 32–34. Parents should read each page to students.

Week 4, Day 3

I. CIRCLE TIME

Read "O is for Out" on page 30. Complete page 29 sections:

- The Starting Point
- Bible Bits
- Let's Talk
- Always Remember

II. STUFF TO DO

Complete "O is for Out" coloring sheet. Use student's copy in this PLP page 152. See page 29 for Stuff to Do.

III. QUICK REVIEW

See page 29. Go deeper for older students on page 62.

IV. NOAH'S ARK PRE-SCHOOL ACTIVITY BOOK

Complete pages 35–37. Parents should read each page to students.

Week 4, Day 4

I. CIRCLE TIME

Read "P is for Pleasure" on page 32. Complete page 31 sections:

- The Starting Point
- Bible Bits
- Let's Talk
- Always Remember

II. STUFF TO DO

Complete "P is for Pleasure" coloring sheet. Use student's copy in this PLP page 153. See page 31 for Stuff to Do.

III. QUICK REVIEW

See page 31. Go deeper for older students on page 63.

IV. NOAH'S ARK PRE-SCHOOL ACTIVITY BOOK

Complete pages 38–39. Parents should read each page to students.

N is for Noah (*N is for Noah* pages 33-40 and Notes pages 63-65)

Week 5, Day 1

I. CIRCLE TIME
Read "Q is for Quiet" on page 34. Complete page 33 sections:

- The Starting Point
- Bible Bits
- Let's Talk
- Always Remember

II. STUFF TO DO
Complete "Q is for Quiet" coloring sheet. Use student's copy in this PLP page 154. See page 33 for Stuff to Do.

III. QUICK REVIEW
See page 33. Go deeper for older students on page 64.

IV. NOAH'S ARK PRE-SCHOOL ACTIVITY BOOK
Complete pages 40–41. Parents should read each page to students.

Week 5, Day 2

I. CIRCLE TIME
Read "R is for Raven" on page 36. Complete page 35 sections:

- The Starting Point
- Bible Bits
- Let's Talk
- Always Remember

II. STUFF TO DO
Complete "R is for Raven" coloring sheet. Use student's copy in this PLP page 155. See page 35 for Stuff to Do.

III. QUICK REVIEW
See page 35. Go deeper for older students on page 64.

IV. NOAH'S ARK PRE-SCHOOL ACTIVITY BOOK
Complete pages 42–43. Parents should read each page to students.

Week 5, Day 3

I. CIRCLE TIME
Read "S is for Sent" on page 38. Complete page 37 sections:

- The Starting Point
- Bible Bits
- Let's Talk
- Always Remember

II. STUFF TO DO
Complete "S is for Sent" coloring sheet. Use student's copy in this PLP page 156. See page 37 for Stuff to Do.

III. QUICK REVIEW
See page 37. Go deeper for older students on page 65.

IV. NOAH'S ARK PRE-SCHOOL ACTIVITY BOOK
Complete pages 44–45. Parents should read each page to students.

Week 5, Day 4

I. CIRCLE TIME
Read "T is for Twice" on page 40. Complete page 39 sections:

- The Starting Point
- Bible Bits
- Let's Talk
- Always Remember

II. STUFF TO DO
Complete "T is for Twice" coloring sheet. Use student's copy in this PLP page 157. See page 39 for Stuff to Do.

III. QUICK REVIEW
See page 39. Go deeper for older students on page 65.

IV. NOAH'S ARK PRE-SCHOOL ACTIVITY BOOK
Complete pages 46–47. Parents should read each page to students.

Week 6, Day 1
I. CIRCLE TIME
Read "U is for Usher" on page 42. Complete page 41 sections:

- The Starting Point
- Bible Bits
- Let's Talk
- Always Remember

II. STUFF TO DO
Complete "U is for Usher" coloring sheet. Use student's copy in this PLP page 158. See page 41 for Stuff to Do. Reference *Dinosaurs By Design*.

III. QUICK REVIEW
See page 41. Go deeper for older students on page 66.

IV. NOAH'S ARK PRE-SCHOOL ACTIVITY BOOK
Complete pages 48–50. Parents should read each page to students.

Week 6, Day 2
I. CIRCLE TIME
Read "V is for Very" on page 44. Complete page 43 sections:

- The Starting Point
- Bible Bits
- Let's Talk
- Always Remember

II. STUFF TO DO
Complete "V is for Very" coloring sheet. Use student's copy in this PLP page 159. See page 43 for Stuff to Do.

III. QUICK REVIEW
See page 43. Go deeper for older students on page 67.

IV. NOAH'S ARK PRE-SCHOOL ACTIVITY BOOK
Complete pages 51–53. Parents should read each page to students.

Week 6, Day 3
I. CIRCLE TIME
Read "W is for Wonderful" on page 46. Complete page 45 sections:

- The Starting Point
- Bible Bits
- Let's Talk
- Always Remember

II. STUFF TO DO
Complete "W is for Wonderful" coloring sheet. Use student's copy in this PLP page 160. See page 45 for Stuff to Do.

III. QUICK REVIEW
See page 45. Go deeper for older students on page 67.

IV. NOAH'S ARK PRE-SCHOOL ACTIVITY BOOK
Complete pages 54–55. Parents should read each page to students.

Week 6, Day 4
I. CIRCLE TIME
Read "X is in eXtensive" on page 48. (Explain: "x" is in the middle.) Complete page 47 sections:

- The Starting Point
- Bible Bits
- Let's Talk
- Always Remember

II. STUFF TO DO
Complete "X is in eXtensive" coloring sheet. Use student's copy in this PLP page 161. See page 47 for Stuff to Do. Reference *Dinosaurs By Design*.

III. QUICK REVIEW
See page 47. Go deeper for older students on page 68.

IV. NOAH'S ARK PRE-SCHOOL ACTIVITY BOOK
Complete pages 56–57. Parents should read each page to students.

Week 7, Day 1

I. CIRCLE TIME

Read "Y is for Years" on page 50. Complete page 49 sections:

- The Starting Point
- Bible Bits
- Let's Talk
- Always Remember

II. STUFF TO DO

Complete "Y is for Years" coloring sheet. Use student's copy in this PLP page 162. See page 49 for Stuff to Do.

III. QUICK REVIEW

See page 49. Go deeper for older students on page 68.

IV. NOAH'S ARK PRE-SCHOOL ACTIVITY BOOK

Complete pages 58–59. Parents should read each page to students.

Week 7, Day 2

I. CIRCLE TIME

Read "Z is for Zealous" on page 52. Complete page 51 sections:

- The Starting Point
- Bible Bits
- Let's Talk
- Always Remember

II. STUFF TO DO

Complete "Z is for Zealous" coloring sheet. Use student's copy in this PLP page 163. See page 51 for Stuff to Do.

III. QUICK REVIEW

See page 51. Go deeper for older students on page 69.

IV. NOAH'S ARK PRE-SCHOOL ACTIVITY BOOK

Complete pages 60–61. Parents should read each page to students.

Week 7, Day 3

I. CIRCLE TIME

Read *N is for Noah* pages 2–52.

Work with student to memorize what each letter of the alphabet in *N is for Noah* stands for. The instructor should say the name of the letter and let the student say what it stands for. Older students may be able say both the letter and what it stands for while going through the alphabet.

II. NOAH'S ARK PRE-SCHOOL ACTIVITY BOOK

Complete pages 62–63. Parents should read each page to students.

Week 7, Day 4

I. CIRCLE TIME

Read *N is for Noah* pages 2–52.

Continue to work with the student to memorize what each letter of the alphabet in *N is for Noah* stands for. The instructor should say the name of the letter and let the student say what it stands for. Older students may be able say both the letter and what it stands for while going through the alphabet.

II. NOAH'S ARK PRE-SCHOOL ACTIVITY BOOK

Complete pages 64–66. Parents should read each page to students.

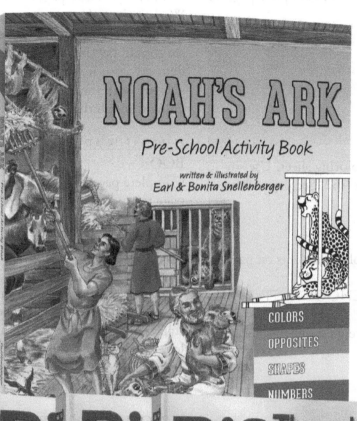

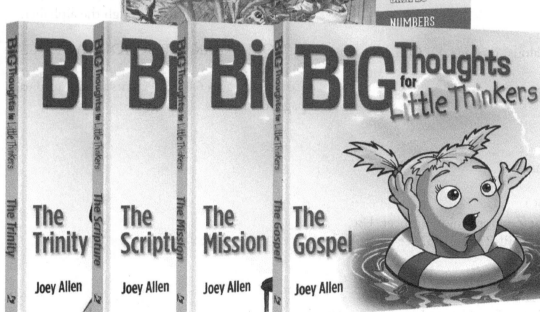

Week 1, Day 1

I. CIRCLE TIME

Parents: Read the Foreword and "A Word to Parents and Teachers" in the book *Big Thoughts for Little Thinkers: The Scripture* to yourself before beginning the lesson with students.

Read the first 13 pages of *Big Thoughts for Little Thinkers: The Scripture*. (The last page for today begins with "People who believed. . . .") As you read each page:

- Ask the student to repeat what the page says.

- Take a few minutes to discuss the topic.

- Teach students how a Bible study is done by looking up and reading each Scripture reference. (Parents may wish to select one per page or one every couple of pages.)

- Ask student to repeat each Scripture reference.

II. NOAH'S ARK PRE-SCHOOL ACTIVITY BOOK

Complete pages 67–69. Parents should read each page to students. Ask students what other words they learned in *A is for Adam, D is for Dinosaur*, and *N is for Noah* for each letter.

Week 1, Day 2

I. CIRCLE TIME

Read the last 14 pages of *Big Thoughts for Little Thinkers: The Scripture*. (The first page for today begins with "God used about. . . .") As you read each page:

- Ask the student to repeat what the page says.

- Take a few minutes to discuss the topic.

- Teach students how a Bible study is done by looking up and reading each Scripture reference. (Parents may wish to select one per page or one every couple of pages.)

- Ask student to repeat each Scripture reference.

- Review the concepts of *Big Thoughts for Little Thinkers: The Scripture*.

II. NOAH'S ARK PRE-SCHOOL ACTIVITY BOOK

Complete pages 70–73. Parents should read each page to students. Ask students what other words they learned in *A is for Adam, D is for Dinosaur*, and *N is for Noah* for each letter.

Week 1, Day 3

I. CIRCLE TIME

Parents: Read the Foreword and "A Word to Parents and Teachers" in the book *Big Thoughts for Little Thinkers: The Gospel* to yourself before beginning the lesson with students.

Read the first 13 pages of *Big Thoughts for Little Thinkers: The Gospel*. (The last page for today begins with "Jesus is alive. . . .") As you read each page:

- Ask the student to repeat what the page says.

- Take a few minutes to discuss the topic.

- Teach students how a Bible study is done by looking up and reading each Scripture reference. (Parents may wish to select one per page or one every couple of pages.)

- Ask student to repeat each Scripture reference.

II. NOAH'S ARK PRE-SCHOOL ACTIVITY BOOK

Complete pages 74–76. Parents should read each page to students. Ask students what other words they learned in *A is for Adam, D is for Dinosaur*, and *N is for Noah* for each letter.

Week 1, Day 4

I. CIRCLE TIME

Parents: Read the Foreword and "Afterword for Parents and Teachers" in the book *Big Thoughts for Little Thinkers: The Gospel* to yourself before beginning the lesson with students.

Read the last 13 pages of *Big Thoughts for Little Thinkers: The Gospel*. (The first page for today begins with "Many people think. . . .") As you read each page:

- Ask the student to repeat what the page says.

- Take a few minutes to discuss the topic.

- Teach students how a Bible study is done by looking up and reading each Scripture reference. (Parents may wish to select one per page or one every couple of pages.)

- Ask student to repeat each Scripture reference.

- Review the concepts of *Big Thoughts for Little Thinkers: The Gospel.*

II. NOAH'S ARK PRE-SCHOOL ACTIVITY BOOK

Complete pages 77–79. Parents should read each page to students. Ask students what other words they learned in *A is for Adam, D is for Dinosaur,* and *N is for Noah* for each letter.

Big Thoughts

Week 2, Day 1

I. CIRCLE TIME

Parents: Read the Foreword and "A Word to Parents and Teachers" in the book *Big Thoughts for Little Thinkers: The Mission* to yourself before beginning the lesson with students.

Read the first 13 pages of *Big Thoughts for Little Thinkers: The Mission.* (The last page for today begins with "Jesus showed God's love. . . .") As you read each page:

- Ask the student to repeat what the page says.

- Take a few minutes to discuss the topic.

- Teach students how a Bible study is done by looking up and reading each Scripture reference. (Parents may wish to select one per page or one every couple of pages.)

- Ask student to repeat each Scripture reference.

II. NOAH'S ARK PRE-SCHOOL ACTIVITY BOOK

Complete pages 80–82. Parents should read each page to students. Ask students what other words they learned in *A is for Adam, D is for Dinosaur,* and *N is for Noah* for each letter.

Week 2, Day 2

I. CIRCLE TIME

Read the last 14 pages of *Big Thoughts for Little Thinkers: The Mission.* (The first page for today begins with "Jesus did what. . . .") As you read each page:

- Ask the student to repeat what the page says.

- Take a few minutes to discuss the topic.

- Teach students how a Bible study is done by looking up and reading each Scripture reference. (Parents may wish to select one per page or one every couple of pages.)

- Ask student to repeat each Scripture reference.

- Review the concepts of *Big Thoughts for Little Thinkers: The Mission.*

II. NOAH'S ARK PRE-SCHOOL ACTIVITY BOOK

Complete pages 83–87. Parents should read each page to students.

Week 2, Day 3

I. CIRCLE TIME

Parents: Read the Foreword and "A Word to Parents and Teachers" in the book *Big Thoughts for Little Thinkers: The Trinity* to yourself before beginning the lesson with students.

Read the first 13 pages of *Big Thoughts for Little Thinkers: The Trinity*. (The last page for today begins with "The Father, Son, and Holy Spirit live. . . .") As you read each page:

- Ask the student to repeat what the page says.

- Take a few minutes to discuss the topic.

- Teach students how a Bible study is done by looking up and reading each Scripture reference. (Parents may wish to select one per page or one every couple of pages.)

- Ask student to repeat each Scripture reference.

II. NOAH'S ARK PRE-SCHOOL ACTIVITY BOOK

Complete pages 88–91. Parents should read each page to students. Practice the "Letters of the Alphabet" poem on page 91 until student has memorized it.

Week 2, Day 4

I. CIRCLE TIME

Read the last 11 pages of *Big Thoughts for Little Thinkers: The Trinity*. (The first page for today begins with "Because God is Trinity. . . .") As you read each page:

- Ask the student to repeat what the page says.

- Take a few minutes to discuss the topic.

- Teach students how a Bible study is done by looking up and reading each Scripture reference. (Parents may wish to select one per page or one every couple of pages.)

- Ask student to repeat each Scripture reference.

- Review the concepts of *Big Thoughts for Little Thinkers: The Trinity*.

Parents: Read "The Constantinopolitan Creed of A.D. 381" at the end of *Big Thoughts for Little Thinkers: The Trinity*. You may read and discuss this creed with your student if desired.

II. NOAH'S ARK PRE-SCHOOL ACTIVITY BOOK

Complete pages 92–96. Parents should read each page to students. Practice the "Letters of the alphabet" poem on page 91 until student has memorized it. Have the student recite the poem to the family.

Coloring
Pages

God Creates LIGHT

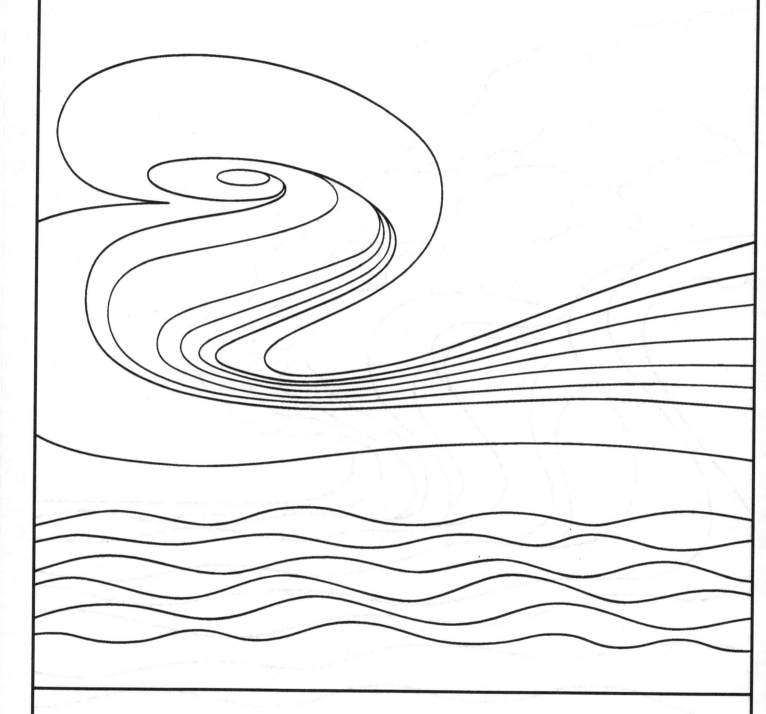

"In the beginning, God created the heaven and the earth...
And God said, 'Let there be light.' And there was light.
And God saw the light, that it was good" (Genesis 1:1, 3-5 KJV).

God said, "Let there be a firmament in the midst of the waters, and let it divide the waters (above) from the waters (below) (Genesis 1:6–8 KJV).

God Creates WATER

God said, "Let the water under the heaven be gathered together unto one place and let the dry land appear: and it was so. And God saw that it was good" (Genesis 1:9–10 KJV).

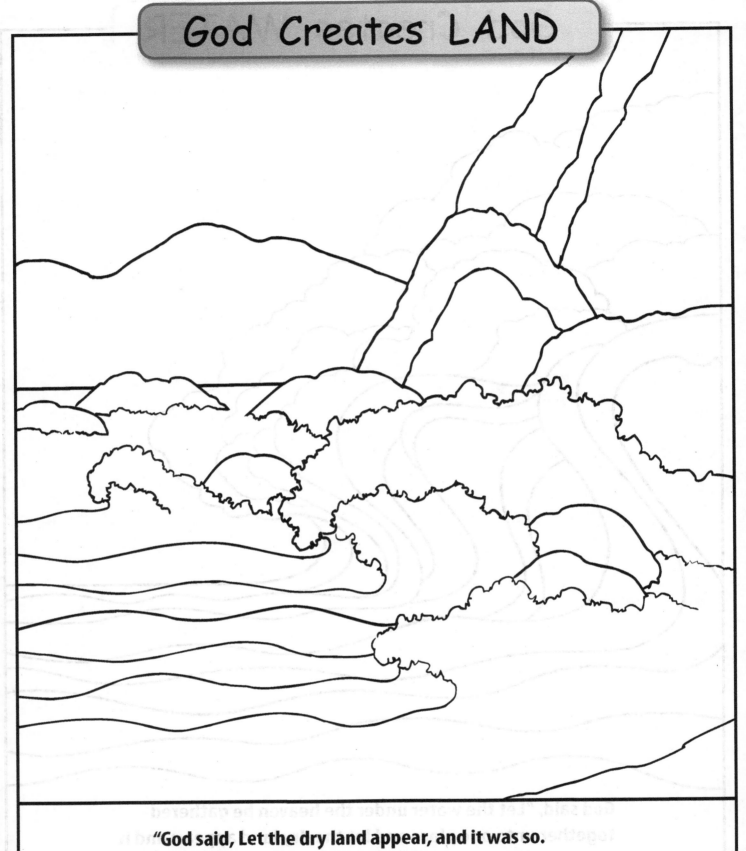

"God said, Let the dry land appear, and it was so. God called the dry land Earth; And God saw that it was good" (Genesis 1:9-10 KJV).

God Creates PLANTS

"And God said, 'Let the bring forth grass, the herb yielding seed, and the fruit tree yielding fruit after his kind... and it was so... and God saw that it was good" (Genesis 1:11-13 KJV).

"And God said, Let there be lights… to divide the day from the night; and let them be for signs, and for seasons…. And let them… give light upon the earth" (Genesis 1:16–18 KJV).

God Creates SEA CREATURES

"God said, 'Let the waters bring forth abundantly the moving creatures'... and God created great whales... after their kind... And God blessed them, saying, Be fruitful, and multiply, and fill the waters in the sea" (Genesis 1:20-22 KJV).

God Creates BIRDS

"And God created... every winged fowl after his kind: and God saw that it was good. And God blessed them, saying, Be fruitful, and multiply, and... let fowl multiply in the earth" (Genesis 1:20, 22 KJV).

Give each child a set
of five circle birds to
color and cut out.
Glue each bird on
a flat wooden stick.
Have children hold up the right
number of birds
while the rhyme is read.

God Creates ANIMALS

"God said, 'Let the earth bring forth the living creature after his kind, cattle, and creeping thing, and beast of the earth after his kind: and it was so" (Genesis 1:24 KJV).

"The Lord God formed man of the dust of the ground, and breathed into his nostrils the breath of life; and man became a living soul" (Genesis 2:7, 22 KJV).

God Creates a Day of Rest

"And on the seventh day God ended his work which he had made; and he rested on the seventh day... And God blessed the seventh day, and sanctified it: because that in it he had rested from all his work" (Genesis 2:2-3 KJV).

God Created ME

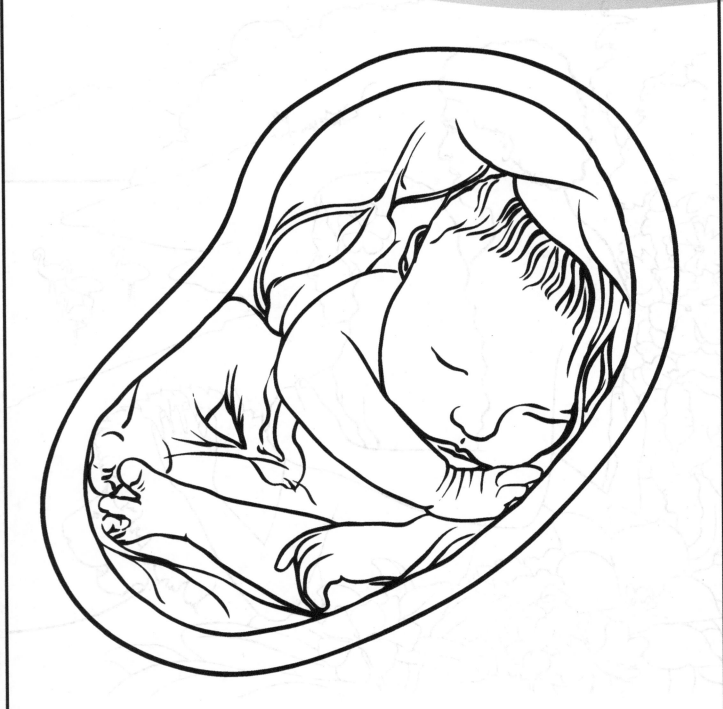

"O Lord, thou hast searched me, and known me... thou hast covered me in my mother's womb. I will praise thee; for I am fearfully and wonderfully made"

(Psalm 139:1, 13, 14 KJV).

The Lord Is My Creator

Supplies Needed: colored pencils, scissors, tape or glue, assorted yarn or ribbon, a coat hanger for each child

1. Color the figures in the boxes (pg 79). Color oval sign (above).

2. Cut out the rectangle figures on the SOLID lines.

3. Fold the images in the rectangles with DOTTED lines.

4. Tape or glue 6" of ribbon in the fold of the double images. Tape the folded images back to back.

5. Use yarn or ribbon to attach images to a coat hanger at different lengths.

6. Hang the oval sign "The Lord Is My Creator" in the middle of the hanger as seen on the illustration above.

Team up with a partner and share your mobile.
Tell WHICH parts of Creation are pictured on your mobile.

The Lord Is My Creator

Supplies Needed: colored pencils, scissors, tape or glue, assorted yarn or ribbon, a coat hanger for each child

1. Color the figures in the boxes (pp. 79). Color oval sign (above).

2. Cut out the rectangle figures on the SOLID lines.

3. Fold the images in the rectangles with DOTTED lines.

4. Tape or glue a 6" of ribbon in the fold of the double images; tape the folded images together.

5. Use yarn or ribbon to attach images to a coat hanger at different lengths.

6. Hang the oval sign "The Lord Is My Creator" in the middle of the hanger, as seen on the illustration above.

Team up with a partner and share your mobile. Tell WHICH parts of creation are pictured on your mobile.

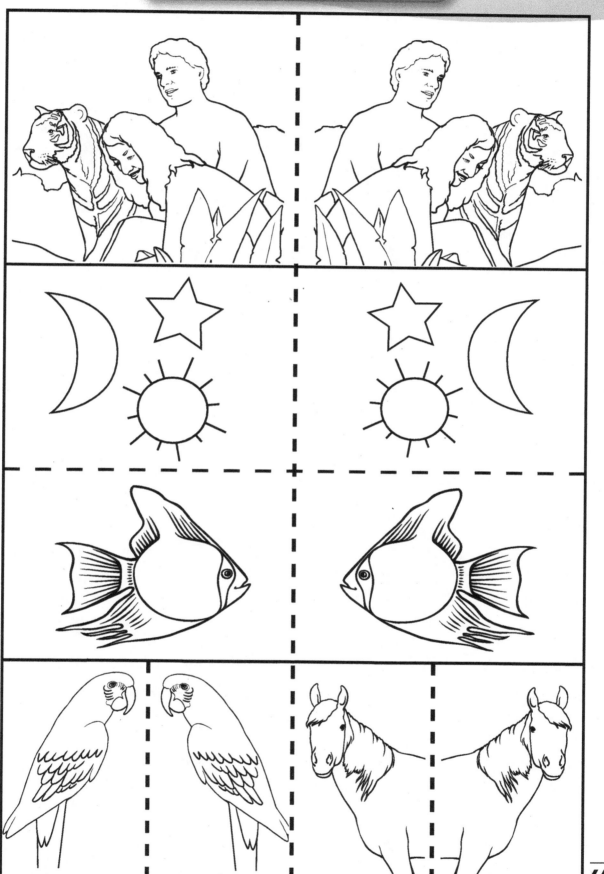

Celebrate Creation

"The earth is the Lord's, and the fullness thereof,
the world, and they that dwell therein" (Psalms 24:1 KJV).

A is for **Adam;** God made him from dust.   Although some scientists don't think it was so,

He wasn't a monkey, he looked just like us.   It was God who was there, and He ought to know.

B is for **Bible**, a book God did give,

to tell where we came from and how we should live.

We did not evolve, God made it so plain,

people are people; we stay just the same.

"My name is _____.

I am made in the God's image.

I am not an animal."

People	Animals	Plants

C is for **Creatures**; God made them all, some rather little, but others quite tall.

He said unto Adam, "What names do you think?" Adam then named them, quick as a wink!

D is for **Dinosaur**, Dodo and Deer,

Like all of the animals, no man did they fear.

But even though all was in true harmony,

Adam then realized, "There's no one like me!"

E is for **Eve**, his beautiful bride,

God made just for Adam, from part of his side.

To sleep God did put him, and when he awoke,

"She's flesh of my flesh," were the words that he spoke.

F is for **Fruit**, God said not to take

"Because if you do, much trouble you'll make!"

They lived in the garden God specially made,

and if they'd obeyed Him, they could have then stayed.

G is for **Ghastly**, for what happened next,

Let's go to the Bible, and look at the text.

In Genesis chapter three and verse one,

Eve met the serpent, but she didn't run.

H is for **How** very sly he did sound,
The Devil saw Eve and the fruit she had found.

"Did God really say, 'Don't eat from that tree?'
It'll open your eyes—you'll be wise, like me."

I is for **Interested**, Eve did become,

she picked off the fruit and then she ate some.

It tasted so nice, what harm could there be?

"Here Adam, eat some and come and join me,"

J is for **Jovial**, as Satan must have been,

The Devil was gleeful with all he had seen.

He was able to trick poor Eve with a lie,

"Obey all my words, and you'll surely not die!"

K is for **Knew**; Adam saw he was bare.

Both he and his wife no clothes they did wear.

They sewed up some fig leaves, and then tried to hide,

as they suddenly realized the Devil had lied.

L is for **Lord**, who reigns up on high,
the one who told Adam, "Obey, or you'll die."

Adam and Eve couldn't hide from their sin,
"Out of my garden, and don't come back in!"

M is for **Moan,** what a mess sin did make.

Thorns, thistles and death, and cursed ground for man's sake.

God had to judge sin. He's so holy and pure,

But God is so good, He provided a cure.

N is for **Never**, no more could they go,

back to the garden, where rivers did flow.

Angels with sword now stood at the gate,

what was in store, and what was their fate?

O is for **Offering**, an animal was killed.

Because of their sin, blood had to be spilled.

But over and over this had to be done,

till Christ on the cross the victory had won.

CREATION   FALL   CURSE   WATER JUDGMENT   CROSS

P is for **Plan**, which God always had,

because he knew man, would turn very bad.

A few thousand years later, God's Son came to be,

a wonderful Savior for you and for me.

CROSS

RESURRECTION

FIRE
JUDGMENT

NEW HEAVENS &
NEW EARTH

HELL

Q is for **Quiet**, Adam and Eve must have been,

when God spoke the words, of Genesis three verse fifteen.

God's Son came to die and be raised from the dead,

so to Hell we'd not go, but to Heaven instead.

R is for **Rough**, how life had become,

the effects of God's curse had really begun.

Adam worked hard to obtain food to eat,

he made lots of sweat, so he must have been beat!

Cut out each image. Place in a pile, arrange them in two stacks – one for the history of the world, the other the points of salvations and a new earth. Then ask the student to put each in sequence in the correct order in each stack and explain what is happening in each.

WATER JUDGMENT

FALL

CREATION

CURSE

CROSS

RESURRECTION

CROSS

HELL

JUDGMENT

NEW HEAVENS & NEW EARTH

S is for **Seventy**, and maybe lots more,
Imagine their family with children galore.

Long before Moses, when people were few,
brothers and sisters could marry, that's true!

T is for **Trouble**, oh, such a sad day,

Cain struck brother Abel, and dead there he lay.

The Lord punished Cain for what he had done,

but things still got worse, there was much more to come.

U is for **Utterly** shocking and bad.

People were killing, it became quite a fad!

God said, "That's enough! The world I will judge."

He sent a great flood—which made lots of sludge.

V is for **Violent**, were the waters of the flood,

people and animals were buried in the mud.

But God saved Noah, wife, daughters and sons,

along with the animals in an ark weighing tons.

W is for **Walk**; they came out of the ark.

The world was so different, the Flood left its mark.

Had people now learnt God's Word to obey?

They certainly did not, it is so sad to say.

X is for **eXplode**, the population sure grew,

but what happened next, read God's Word for the clue.
They built a great tower to reach to the sky,
for God's spoken Word, they were quick to defy.

Y is for **Yes**, God did soon judge their sin,
by confusing their language—what a terrible din!

He scattered the people all over the place,
till God's final judgment, we'll all have to face.

109

Z is for **Zip**, so quick it will be,
when Jesus comes back for you and for me.

If our name is found in the "Lamb's Book of Life,"
We'll sure live forever in a place with no strife.

In the beginning God created the heavens and the earth...

A is for Answers from God's Holy Book;
Just open the pages and take a good look.

God created the earth, in space it did hang;
Creation's first day, without a BIG BANG.

B is for Bible, where it says on day 2,

God made the clean air for me and for you.

He divided the waters above and below;

Day 3 comes next, so there we shall go.

C is for Continent, the first dry land,

Which God had made by His Powerful hand.

Then He commanded that all the plants grow;

The third day was truly a beautiful show.

D is for Dinosaur, but you'll have to wait,

'Cause on day four other things God did make.

He formed the sun, the stars, and the moon.

Are you ready? We'll see those dinosaurs soon!

E is for Everything that swims in the seas,

Made on day five, with the birds in the trees.

He also created the great Plesiosaur;

Reading God's Word, we can know this for sure.

F is for Fantastic – that's all we can say,

As we see what God made on this, the sixth day!

Adam and Eve and the pouched kangaroo;

The rest of the animals and dinosaurs, too.

G is for the Garden God specially made,

Where Adam and Eve could always have stayed.

Living in Eden, a world without sin;

What a beautiful place for them to live in.

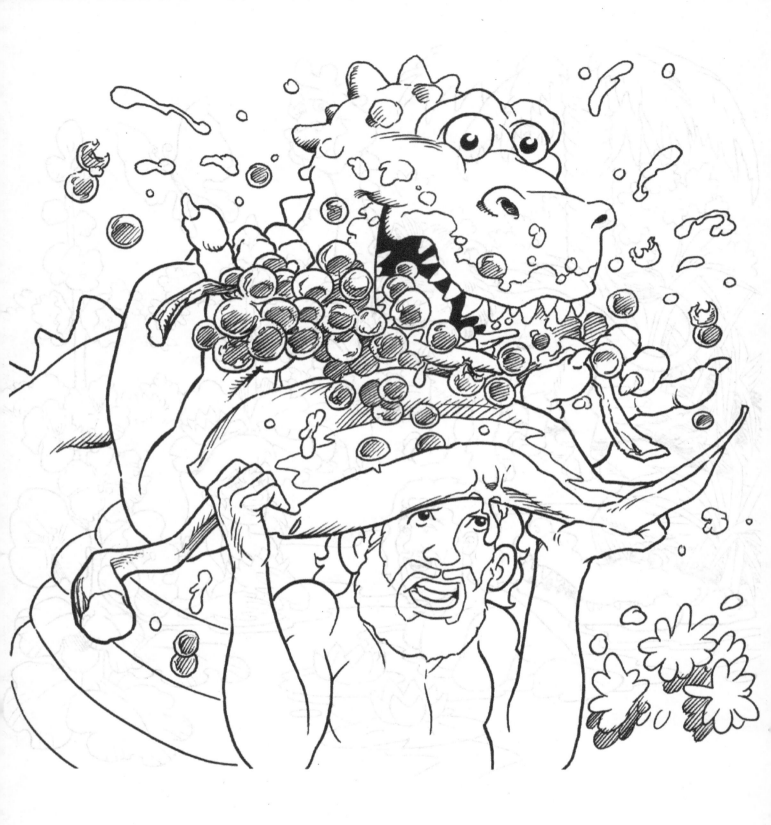

H is for Hungry, it's how we describe   Adam wasn't scared to watch dinosaurs eat,

A big dinosaur with his mouth open wide.   Because all the creatures ate plants, and not meat.

I is the letter in the middle of sIn,
To remind us all of the trouble we're in.

Dinosaurs, people, and the whole universe;
Because of man's sin, God judged with a curse.

J means Just awful – I'm sure we could say

The effects of sin grew worse every day.

Flesh became violent, the Bible reveals.

Were people and creatures now dinosaur meals?

K is for Knowledge, which made Noah sad;

The world would be judged, because people were bad!

God warned he would send a terrible flood

That would cover the world with water and mud.

L is for Listen: Noah knew that he should,

As soon as God said, "Make an ark out of wood.

Take each land animal, two-by-two;

Your family's among the hard-working crew."

M is for Monster like the great dinosaur;

But how could he enter the ark through the door?

Well, many dinosaurs were really quite small;

The young ones, especially, were not very tall.

N is for Noah, his wife, and his kin,

Who, with the animals, also went in.

Dinosaurs outside the ark were all drowned;

That's why as fossils their bones are now found.

O is for Out of the ark they all ran,

Once the huge vessel came safely to land.

Stegasaurs, lambeosaurs, nodosaurs, and more;

After the Flood there were dinosaurs galore!

Apatosaurus

Iguanodon

Tyrannosaurus

Triceratops

P is for Pronounce: are the names hard for you?

Iguanodon, diplodocus, now how did you do?

Brachiosaurus, tyrannosaurus, and others as well,

What happened to them is the story we'll tell.

Q is for Question – why can't we any more,

Look around and see even one dinosaur?

They're surely all dead, it's as simple as that;

Try to guess why – put on your thinking hat.

R is for Reasons – perhaps there are more;

After the Flood, times were tougher for sure;

Volcanoes and storms, then drought and snow,

Maybe people killed them – they frightened them so.

S is for a Section from God's Holy Book;

About a great beast; when he walked the ground shook.

Behemoth, or monster, was this animal's name:

Our word "dinosaur" means almost the same.

T is for Tales that we often hear
About terrible dragons that made men fear.

Maybe these tales could actually be
Stories of dinosaurs men used to see.

U is for Understand, which we want to do;

The Bible explains the dinosaurs for you.

It also tells how from sin to be saved;

By trusting in Jesus, who rose from the grave.

Adam and Eve

Jonah

David and Goliath

Jesus

If I have told you earthly things, and and ye believe not,

how shall ye believe, if I tell you of heavenly things? John 3:12

V is for how Very much we can say
We all should read the Bible each day.

Dinosaurs we've proven, are no mystery;
God's Word teaches us true history.

W is for Watchfulness, which we should all learn,   He's going to judge this world once again;

Since some day Jesus, our Lord, will return.   But this time by fire, instead of by rain.

X is in eXcited, which Christians should be,

One day we know that heaven we'll see.

There'll be no more dying, or crying or pain;

For God our Creator, forever will reign.

Y is for Years, how long could it be,

Since God made the world for you and for me?

"Probably only six thousand or so,"

Say many good scientists; they ought to know!

Z is for the Zeal which people should see,

As we tell the truth about history.

The dinosaurs certainly have not evolved;

Through God's Holy Word, the puzzle is solved!

I hereby declare that I am going to live with Jesus forever because I have repented of my sin, which I inherited from Adam and continue to do personally. I also declare that I love and trust the Lord Jesus with all my heart and soul and believe in Him. I know this is true because Jesus died for my sin, and conquered death because He rose from the dead. I know this because the Bible tells me. I declare that I am a Christian.

Name _____

Date _____

A is for Ark

Ark is a name for a great big boat.

It had to be strong so it could float

To survive many months during a global Flood,

'Cause man's rebellion God had to judge.

B is for Back

Back in a garden is when it began,
When the saddest day was caused by a man.
Adam was told, "Don't eat from this tree."
God made it clear, "You must obey Me."

C is for Called

Called the saddest day in world history,
Adam disobeyed God and ate from that tree.
Now everything changed – dirt, animals, and man.
Sin entered the world; the rebellion began.

D is for Dreadful

Dreadful things happened—when Cain killed his brother,
Violent things, oh, one after another.
The effects of sin were seen everywhere,
But sadly, so many just didn't even care.

E is for Earth

Earth, moon, and stars – the whole universe
Was suffering the effects of an awful Curse.
Disease, death, and suffering, and lots of pain,
Nothing would ever be quite just the same.

F is for Fruitful

"Be fruitful and multiply," the first two were told.
They probably had fifty by the time they were old.
Their children had children and then there were more,
Hundreds of years later, there were people galore.

G is for Grave

Grave is the situation many years after creation.
At the time of Noah lived a wicked generation.
All but eight people they jeered and they scoffed;
They didn't love God, all they did was just mock.

H is for Hear

Hear that great task that God said to do:
Build a great boat – your family's the crew.
Noah obeyed, he loved God so much,
He didn't complain or make any fuss.

I is for Insane

Insane is the word that some may have used;

"Old Noah's stupid," some may have accused.

Noah must've been sad 'cause he knew what God said.

It wouldn't be long and these people would be dead.

J is for Judgment

Judgment by water, God revealed His plan,
A global Flood would destroy the land.
That's why Noah a big ship had to make,
It was called an ark, with a barge-like shape.

K is for Kept

Kept safe on the ark, only eight people went on board,
With each kind of land animal and food that was stored.
For seven days the ark stood with the door open wide,
Noah must have pleaded, "Please, people, please come inside."

L is for Laughing

Laughing and scoffing Noah must have been hearing

As he pleaded with people, "God's judgment you be fearing.

My family and each kind of land animal's inside.

There's still plenty of room and the door's open wide."

M is for Mighty

Mighty must've been the bang when God closed the door,
As the land did shake and the heavens did roar,
Great fountains of water broke through the ground
And rain came down with a deafening sound.

N is for Noah

Noah, now he's a man that sure stood out
As he trusted God's Word, without any doubt.
What a great man of God Noah must have been;
He believed God's Word about things unseen.

O is for Over

Over all of the earth the water flowed fast;
For many, many months this judgment would last.
People outside the ark would have died;
Too late they realized that God had not lied.

P is for Pleasure

Pleasure is not how God viewed this great Flood.

He must have been sad to see people die in the mud.

They could have gone through the door to be saved;

A way of salvation for them God had paved.

Q is for Quiet

Quiet must have been Noah and his family
When all of the destruction outside they did see.
But then they must have praised God out loud,
No doubt they humbly prayed with heads bowed.

R is for Raven

Raven was the first bird Noah sent from the boat,
Now that the ark no longer did float.
God caused the water to drain off the land
And dried up the earth using wind like a fan.

S is for Sent

Sent from the ark, the raven did fly
To and fro across the sky.
So Noah sent out a dove as a test,
But it came back so it could rest.

T is for Twice

Twice, Noah chose the dove to fly about
To see if from the ark they could finally go out.
When the dove came back with a leaf from a tree
Noah knew now soon the earth he would see.

U is for Usher

"Usher out of the ark," God to Noah did tell,
"Your family and each of the animals as well."
Noah obeyed, as he always had.
To get out of the ark, he must have been glad.

V is for Very

Very thankful was Noah, he was full of praise.

So to thank the Lord, an altar he raised.

He made a great sacrifice, the best he could do,

For God saved Noah, His Word is so true.

W is for Wonderful

Wonderful, magnificent, and beautiful was the sign
When the colors of the rainbow overhead did shine.
It was God's promise that there will never be
Another global Flood like this catastrophe.

X is in eXtensive

eXtensive, a word that describes evidence of the Flood,
Fossils over the world that were buried in mud.
What a warning to remind me and you
To be like Noah, believe God's Word is true.

Y is for Years

Years, about four thousand three hundred are there,
Since the worldwide Flood made the earth so bare.
And another judgment's coming, from God's Word we learn,
When the whole of the universe from fire will burn.

Z is for Zealous

Zealous, all of us need to be
To tell of God's ark for you and for me.
Jesus, God's Son, did die for our sin.
He is the ark door — make sure you go in.

I hereby declare that I am going to live with Jesus forever because I have repented of my sin, which I inherited from Adam and continue to do personally. I also declare that I love and trust the Lord Jesus with all my heart and soul and believe in Him. I know this is true because Jesus died for my sin, and conquered death because He rose from the dead. I know this because the Bible tells me. I declare that I am a Christian.

Name _____

Date _____

Parent Lesson Plan

Preschool

BIBLICAL BEGINNINGS PRESCHOOL

Ages 3, 4 and 5 year olds

Package Includes: *A is for Adam; A is for Adam DVD; D is for Dinosaur; D is for Dinosaur DVD; N is for Noah; Noah's Ark Pre-School; God Made the World & Me; Dinosaurs Stars of the Show; Big Thoughts for Little Thinkers: The Gospel; The Mission; The Scripture; The Trinity; Creation Story for Children; When Dragons Hearts Were Good; Dinosaur by Design; Biblical Beginnings Pre-school , Parent Lesson Planner*

14 Book, 2 DVD Package
978-0-89051-852-6   **$187.84**

3rd–6th Grade

SCIENCE STARTERS: ELEMENTARY PHYSICAL & EARTH SCIENCE

1 year, Science
3rd – 6th grade

6 Book Package Includes: *Forces & Motion –Student, Student Journal, and Teacher; The Earth – Student, Teacher & Student Journal; Parent Lesson Planner*

6 Book Package
978-0-89051-748-2   **$51.94**

SCIENCE STARTERS: ELEMENTARY GENERAL SCIENCE & ASTRONOMY

1 year, Science
3rd – 6th grade

7 Book Package Includes: *Water & Weather – Student, Student Journal, and Teacher; The Universe – Student, Teacher, & Student Journal; Parent Lesson Planner*

7 Book Package
978-0-89051-816-8   **$54.93**

SCIENCE STARTERS: ELEMENTARY CHEMISTRY & PHYSICS

1 year, Science
3rd – 6th grade

7 Book Package Includes: *Matter – Student, Student Journal, and Teacher; Energy – Student, Teacher, & Student Journal; Parent Lesson Planner*

7 Book Package
978-0-89051-749-9   **$54.93**

ELEMENTARY GEOGRAPHY AND CULTURES

1 year, Geography
3rd – 6th grade

Package Includes: *Children's Atlas of God's World, Passport to the World, & Parent Lesson Planner*

3 Book Package
978-0-89051-814-4   **$49.97**

ELEMENTARY BIBLE AND ENGLISH GRAMMAR

1 year, Grammar/Bible
3rd – 6th grade

Package Includes: *Illustrated Family Bible Stories & Parent Lesson Planner*

2 Book Package
978-0-89051-852-6   **$39.98**

ELEMENTARY WORLD HISTORY

1 year, History
3rd – 6th

Package Includes: *The Big Book of History; Noah's Ark: Thinking Outside the Box (book and DVD); & Parent Lesson Planner*

3 Book, 1 DVD Package
978-0-89051-815-1   **$64.96**

ELEMENTARY ZOOLOGY

1 year, Zoology
4th – 6th

Package Includes: *World of Animals; Dinosaur Activity Book; The Complete Aquarium Adventure; The Complete Zoo Adventure; Parent Lesson Planner*

5 Book Package
978-0-89051-747-5   **$85.95**

7th–9th Grade

INTRO TO OCEANOGRAPHY & ECOLOGY

1 year, Science
7th – 9th grade
½ Credit

Package Includes: *The Ocean Book; The Ecology Book; Parent Lesson Planner*

3 Book Package
978-0-89051-754-3   **$45.97**

GEOLOGY & BIBLICAL HISTORY

1 year, Geology
7th – 9th
1 Credit

Package Includes: *Explore the Grand Canyon; Explore Yellowstone; Explore Yosemite & Zion National Parks; Your Guide to the Grand Canyon; Your Guide to Yellowstone; Your Guide to Zion & Bryce Canyon National Parks; Parent Lesson Planner.*

4 Book, 3 DVD Package
978-0-89051-750-5   **$108.93**

INTRO TO ARCHAEOLOGY & GEOLOGY

1 year, Geology
7th – 9th
½ Credit

Package Includes: *The Archaeology Book; The Geology Book; Parent Lesson Planner*

3 Book Package
978-0-89051-751-2   **$45.97**

MasterBooks.com
Where Faith Grows!

Parent Lesson Plan

CHRISTIAN HISTORY: BIOGRAPHIES OF FAITH

1 year, Church
7th – 9th grade
1 Credit

Package Includes: *Life of John Newton, Life of Washington, Life of Andrew Jackson, Life of John Knox, Life of Luther,* & *Parent Lesson Planner*

6 Book Package
978-0-89051-847-2 **$101.94**

CONCEPTS OF MATHEMATICS & PHYSICS

1 year, Physics
7th – 9th grade
½ Credit

Package Includes: *Exploring the World of Mathematics; Exploring the World of Physics; Parent Lesson Planner*

3 Book Package
978-0-89051-757-4 **$40.97**

APPLIED SCIENCE: STUDIES OF GOD'S DESIGN IN NATURE

1 year, Engineering
7th – 9th grade
1 Credit

Package Includes: *Made in Heaven, Champions of Invention, Discovery of Design,* & *Parent Lesson Planner*

4 Book Package
978-0-89051-812-0 **$50.96**

INTRO TO METEOROLOGY & ASTRONOMY

1 year, Science
7th – 9th grade
½ Credit

Package Includes: *The Weather Book; The New Astronomy Book; Parent Lesson Planner*

3 Book Package
978-0-89051-753-6 **$45.97**

INTRO TO ASTRONOMY

1 year, Astronomy
7th – 9th grade
½ Credit

Package Includes: *The Stargazer's Guide to the Night Sky; Parent Lesson Planner*

2 Book Package
978-0-89051-760-4 **$47.98**

CONCEPTS OF BIOGEOLOGY & ASTRONOMY

1 year, Science
7th – 9th grade
½ Credit

Package Includes: *Exploring the World Around You, Exploring the World of Astronomy,* & *Parent Lesson Planner*

3 Book Package
978-0-89051-813-7 **$41.97**

CONCEPTS OF EARTH SCIENCE & CHEMISTRY

1 year, Science
7th – 9th grade
½ Credit

Package Includes: *Exploring Planet Earth; Exploring the World of Chemistry; Parent Lesson Planner*

3 Book Package
978-0-89051-755-0 **$40.97**

BASIC PRE-MED

1 year, Biology
8th – 9th grade
½ Credit

Package Includes: *The Genesis of Germs; The Building Blocks in Life Science; Parent Lesson Planner*

3 Book Package
978-0-89051-759-8 **$45.97**

CONCEPTS OF MEDICINE & BIOLOGY

1 year, Science
7th – 9th grade
½ Credit

Package Includes: *Exploring the History of Medicine; Exploring the World of Biology; Parent Lesson Planner*

3 Book Package
978-0-89051-756-7 **$40.97**

INTRO TO SPELEOLOGY & PALEONTOLOGY

1 year, Earth Science
7th – 9th grade
½ Credit

Package Includes: *The Cave Book; The Fossil Book; Parent Lesson Planner*

3 Book Package
978-0-89051-752-9 **$44.97**

THE SCIENCE OF LIFE: BIOLOGY

1 year, Science
8th – 9th grade
½ Credit

Package Includes: *Building Blocks in Science; Building Blocks in Life Science; Parent Lesson Planner*

3 Book Package
978-0-89051-758-1 **$44.97**

LIFE SCIENCE ORIGINS & SCIENTIFIC THEORY

1 year, Life Science
7th – 9th grade
1 Credit

Package Includes: *Evolution: the Grand Experiment, Teacher Guide, DVD; Living Fossils, Teacher Guide, DVD; Parent Lesson Planner*

5 Book, 2 DVD Package
978-0-89051-761-1 **$144.93**

10th–12th Grade

SURVEY OF ASTRONOMY

1 year, Astronomy
10th – 12th grade
1 Credit

Package Includes: *The Stargazers Guide to the Night Sky; Our Created Moon; Taking Back Astronomy; Our Created Moon DVD; Created Cosmos DVD; Parent Lesson Planner*

4 Book, 2 DVD Package
978-0-89051-766-6   **$113.94**

SURVEY OF SCIENCE HISTORY & CONCEPTS

1 year, Science
10th – 12th grade
1 Credit

Package Includes: *The World of Mathematics; The World of Physics; The World of Biology; The World of Chemistry; Parent Lesson Planner*

5 Book Package
978-0-89051-764-2   **$72.99**

SURVEY OF SCIENCE SPECIALTIES

1 year, Science
10th – 12th grade
1 Credit

Package Includes: *The Cave Book; The Fossil Book; The Geology Book; The Archaeology Book; Parent Lesson Planner*

5 Book Package
978-0-89051-765-9   **$81.95**

ADVANCED PRE-MED STUDIES

1 year, Pre-Med
10th – 12th grade
1 Credit

Package Includes: *Building Blocks in Life Science; The Genesis of Germs; Body by Design; Exploring the History of Medicine; Parent Lesson Planner*

5 Book Package
978-0-89051-767-3   **$78.95**

APOLOGETICS IN ACTION

1 year, Apologetics
10th – 12th grade
½ Credit

Package Includes: *How Do I Know the Bible Is True Volumes 1 & 2; Demolishing Supposed Bible Contradictions Volumes 1 & 2; Lesson Parent Planner*

5 Book Package
978-0-89051-848-9   **$70.95**

BIBLICAL ARCHAEOLOGY

1 year, Biblical Archaeology
10th – 12th grade
1 Credit

Package Includes: *Unwrapping the Pharaohs; Unveiling the Kings of Israel; The Archaeology Book; Parent Lesson Planner.*

4 Book Package
978-0-89051-768-0   **$99.96**

CHRISTIAN HERITAGE

1 year, Christian Heritage
9th – 12th grade
1 Credit

Package Includes: *For You They Signed; Lesson Parent Planner*

2 Book Package
978-0-89051-769-7   **$50.98**

CULTURAL ISSUES: CREATION/ EVOLUTION AND THE BIBLE

1 year, Apologetics
10th – 12th grade
½ Credit

Package Includes: *New Answers Book 1; New Answers Book 2; Parent Lesson Planner*

3 Book Package
978-0-89051-846-5   **$44.97**

INTRO TO BIBLICAL GREEK

½ year, Foreign Language
10th – 12th
½ Credit

Package Includes: *It's Not Greek to Me DVD & Parent Lesson Planner*

1 Book, 1 DVD Package
978-0-89051-818-2   **$33.98**

INTRO TO ECONOMICS: MONEY, HISTORY, & FISCAL FAITH

½ year, Economics
10th – 12th
½ Credit

Package Includes: *Bankruptcy of Our Nation, Money Wise DVD, & Parent Lesson Planner*

2 Book, 4 DVD Package
978-0-89051-811-3   **$57.97**

NATURAL SCIENCE THE STORY OF ORIGINS

1 year, Science
10th – 12th grade
½ Credit

Package Includes: *Evolution: The Grand Experiment; Evolution: The Grand Experiment Teacher's Guide, Evolution: The Grand Experiment DVD; Parent Lesson Planner*

3 Book, 1 DVD Package
978-0-89051-762-8   **$71.97**

PALEONTOLOGY: LIVING FOSSILS

1 year, Science
10th – 12th grade
½ Credit

Package Includes: *Living Fossils, Living Fossils Teacher Guide, Living Fossils DVD; Parent Lesson Planner*

3 Book, 1 DVD Package
978-0-89051-763-5   **$66.97**

RELIGIOUS FREEDOM: SOCIAL AND POLITICAL HISTORY

1 year, Intro to Civics
10th – 12th grade
½ Credit

Package Includes: *The History of Religious Liberty-Student Edition; Parent Lesson Planner*

2 Book Package
978-0-89051-883-0   **$51.98**